100+ DIGITAL IDEAS
IN 100 MINUTES

Generate 100+ ideas for Digital Adoption to Grow Your Business

Anirvan Sen

5C Digital Innovation Series

CONTENTS

INTRODUCTION

In my last book **"Right-Fit Digital Strategy to Accelerate Growth"**, I had mentioned that there is a momentous need for every company to become digital to survive in the coming decade. There is a digital tsunami coming. Irrespective of its size, location or industry, companies across the spectrum face the same colossal existential threat. As more of the population get online and technology advances, more businesses will be compelled to conduct businesses through digital platform. The signs are clear and ominous.

But large number of companies are absolutely clueless on where to start? Many of them have their heads deeply buried in the sand. Then, there are others who have highly myopic understanding of digital technologies. And the biggest one is by far the ones who believe that digital transformation is a binary journey. They believe that you can only become a digital company when you have a digital product or service.

Unfortunately, this could not be further from truth. To become a true digital company, a business has to go much beyond having a digital product or service. In fact, having a digital product or a service is not even a pre-requisite anymore. Companies must identify digital ways for their user interactions, they must have digital marketing campaigns, share their knowledge through content marketing, create insightful data from their virtual interactions with their customers and manage infrastructures that are based in the cloud. A company must have a comprehensive 360 approach with enabling technology and new-age digital tools to truly imbibe the spirit of being digital.

In order to help you get a comprehensive view, we have identified 11 critical elements that form the foundation of a digital company. These 11 elements have been combined to form a Digital Adoption Framework (DAF). This framework is the cornerstone of our Digital Ideation approach.

For you and your company to embark on a digital journey and be successful, you must meet certain pre-conditions.

First of all, you must have the right reasons why it must become digital. Too many companies get bedazzled by the glitter of new-age technology. They end up buying the wrong technology or end up spending far too much money on it. On the other side, businesses completely freak out if they don't understand technicalities and as a result, they get into a shutdown mode for new ideas. Either of these conditions are detrimental.

So, you must first start by looking inside your company. You should look at your business strategy and growth (**chapter - stagnant and elusive growth**) , you must acknowledge that there is a "growth" problem (**chapter – it is not my problem**) and you must also, reconcile to the fact that there are global trends that are driving businesses across the board to become digital (**chapter – Business in the 2020s: The 6 Major Trends**). Once you have gone through this diligent process, only then you are truly ready to get started on a digital journey. Any other way will leave you with a half-baked attempt at best.

Once you have met the pre-conditions, you can initiate your ideation process. In this book, we have explained 3 broad topics that can spur digital ideation.

First topic is the illustration and understanding of each of the 11-elements of Digital Adoption Framework (**Chapter – Digital Adoption Framework**). By reviewing and discussing each of these 11-elements, you will get oriented on what and how you can use different digital elements to adopt in your organization.

Once you have got a comprehensive understanding of the Digital Adoption Framework, you must then use the DAF lens to study your existing and potential customers. First you must define different types of users that you can potentially interact in the virtual world (**Chapter – The customer is Who?**) and then undergo a learning process for all different facets of your customer, their emotions, their aspirations and their interactions with you (**Chapter – Customer profile based Ideation**). By studying and reviewing different angles of a customer relationship, you will generate hundreds of ideas that you can adopt through digital medium.

Once you have understood DAF and applied it to understand your interactions with your customers and prospects, that is when you are ready to conduct a "deep" ideation session (**Chapter – 100+ DAF ideas based on 6M+**). Ideation may sound easy, but most companies struggle with it. Once you have generated the first few ideas, you will find that after the initial set, it becomes hard to generate additional ideas. Companies start to struggle after their first 20 ideas. With a bit of concerted effort and focus, companies can get another 10-15 ideas. But after that, it is an uphill battle.

There are two reasons why one must look at generating 100+ ideas. One is that companies need a big repository of ideas to choose from. The bigger the idea pool, the wider their choice. Secondly, by undergoing this mass idea generation, you will not leave any stone unturned and would have comprehensively, reviewed all aspects that can potentially give you digital ideas.

We have used the 6M cause-and-effect tool that is widely used in the LEAN six-sigma world. 6M denotes man, machine, mother nature, material, measurement and method. We have modified this cause-and-effect tool and added a few more aspects to create a wonderful digital ideation tool.

By going through each of the elements explained in the chapter, along with DAF thinking and your customer profile lens, you should be able to generate hundreds if not thousands of ideas that can give you that elusive growth that you have been looking for so desperately.

The book has been structured for a short read. I know that most of you constantly struggle with time. You dont have the time to go through large books. That is why, I have distilled important topics and put them in an easy-to-understand framework that you can read and understand in less than 2 hours.

Last but not least, the concepts and the frameworks are based on years of experience and research, and a constant habit of experimenting with new ideas. All the ideas have been tested many times with various organizations. However, it will be imprudent of me to say that I have seen all the circumstances under which all my ideas will work. As I have been a life-long learner, I would be keen to learn more of these unknown circumstances and constantly, keep improving our frameworks and ideas. Please feel free to reach out to me at anirvan@fifthchrome.com.

With this I wish you all the best, happy reading and may you get 100+ ideas to grow your business.

◆ ◆ ◆

This book is part of a series. More details can be found at our website www.fifthchrome.com. Please visit us to learn more about our books, our workshops and training, as well as resources that we regularly share including tips, templates and expert interviews.

To ask technical questions or to contact, send us an email at info@fifthchrome.com. Just mention the book name in the subject line so it lands with the right team.

CONDITIONS FOR DIGITAL IDEATION

Digital Ideation is the creative process to generate, design, develop and frame new ideas that utilize enabling technologies. This process is undertaken to foster innovation and identify new opportunities by which businesses can create new value either in terms of growth, operational efficiency, employee satisfaction or others.

As with any creative process, ideation also needs adequate conditions to generate the right level of new ideas. So, how will you know if and when you need it? Some companies believe that ideation is a simple exercise and it can be turned on anytime like a radio. Others believe that digital ideation is a good asset to have and should be done after their operational priorities have been addressed. And then there are those who think technology is something that only IT should look at, and it is the IT function's job to come up with new ideas.

Unfortunately, without the right conditions in place, all efforts will remain superficial and cosmetic in approach. Without the right depth, businesses will struggle to discover the relevant opportunities that enabling technologies can unlock for them.

We have identified the existence of three conditions as a good precursor to digital ideation for growth acceleration:
- Compelling reason
- Global trends
- Alignment on a problem

Compelling Reason

Unless they are hungry, lions do not hunt. The same thinking also applies to businesses. Without a compelling reason in place, businesses end up making half-hearted attempts with their strategy. In these half-hearted attempts even, the smallest hurdle can be enough for you to abandon the effort.

Now throw in the technology aspect of the digital world. Only a few understand the underlying complexities. These complexities are usually under the hood and therefore, should not be an area of concern for most people. However, if opened it can appear daunting and can put off many a people.

In general, these objections and resistances do not let new ideas and innovation go much further in their evolution in a business.

However, all these sensibilities change when businesses come across doomsday scenarios staring them in the face. One of the biggest challenges that a business can face is continuous stagnant growth.

It is important to understand that stagnancy is not about growth plateauing for a year or two; it is more like a few successive years. During these low years, the business has tried multiple initiatives and methods but has not been able to make any inroads to growth. This can be due to a stubborn market or perhaps the competition bar is really high. It could also be due to prior failed internal initiatives. A combination of some or all of these elements could also be the cause.

It is here that we say that a business has a compelling enough reason to think digital ideation. Please do not confuse this with using an ERP or buying new servers. Digital ideation is linked with new age business-enabling technology.

Simply put, when a business has run out of other conventional avenues of improvement, it is time for a disruptive change. And that is the right condition for ideation.

Global Trends

Technology has evolved rapidly over the last three decades. But it has seen especially unprecedented change over the past 10 years. And this change is just getting exponentially accelerated. With this change, there is also another reality dawning on us. All businesses must become digital in the next few years. Whether direct products or services through digital medium, or the entire ecosystem of awareness, customer acquisition, order fulfillment and customer experience, most of it is going to be transacted through digital medium.

We have identified six global trends that will accelerate digital evolution in the coming decade:
- Baby boomers and Gen-X approaching retirement
- Covid-19 defining a new normal
- Rapid technology advances
- Millennials' and Gen-Z's influence on work culture
- Shifts in cross-border commerce
- Deconstruction of jobs

All these trends strongly indicate the need for rapid digital adoption. Businesses across the globe need to rethink their strategy. They must firmly figure out how and what digital adoption would they need and how to become a digital company. Unfortunately, the scary part is that those businesses who will not pay heed to these trends are likely to disappear before the decade is out.

Alignment On A Problem

There may be all sorts of indication that the sky is going to fall. Your business refuses to grow despite all the technics and initiatives you have run over the last few years. Blame game is ripe and the market is absolutely merciless for you.

And yet, there does not seem to be a common agenda in your leadership team. New ideas are constantly thwarted by other leaders. At a macro level, most of the leaders understand that your business is facing a gloomy future, there is no consensus on the problem.

And this is the third condition that is a precursor to digital ideation.

You must be able to identify the specific problems that are plaguing your business. And then you should be able to assign accountability to your leadership team on how to explore potential solutions and implementation.

Buy-ins need to be comprehensive, concerns must be identified and resolved. Nay-sayers need to be aligned and risk-averse leaders need to be coached in-order to get a full alignment on a problem thinking.

Over the next three chapters, we will explore these three pre-conditions required for digital ideation in greater detail.

Notes:

- 6 Global Trends: Inspired by Daniel Priestley's workshop on Key Person of Influence

STAGNANT AND ELUSIVE GROWTH

When is the right time for a conventional business to explore an entry into the digital world?

There is no right or universal answer for this question. However, I have seen that without a few compelling reasons being in place, most organizations fail to extend their business into the digital world effectively. Apart from conducting a few scattered discussions or perhaps a couple of experiments that go up to the Proof-of-Concept (PoC) stage, most digital expansion programs never grow wings to fly.

So, what are these compelling reasons?

While I do not claim to have all the answers, in this chapter, I will share some of the more relevant ones that create the optimum conditions for digital ideation. Any of these scenarios below is a good reason to begin on the path to 'informed' digital innovation, and more importantly, to stay with it.

Stagnant Market

First off, if you operate in a market that is saturated, commoditized and has growth lower than overall GDP expansion, you are operating in a category that does not provide any uplift to your business. Industries such as insurance, banking, agriculture, dairy farming, utilities and others fall into this category. A large chunk of the market is controlled by large companies, with only a small component being left for businesses in the unorganized sector. In fact, many small companies in this space operate primarily due to the support of local or national governments. With competition being fierce and margins being razor-thin, the only way to compete in a market such as this would be by undercutting prices — usually not a sustainable strategy for the long-term.

Sluggish Top-Line

With external market conditions being difficult as they are, even internal measures do not seem to have any impact either on revenue growth or on profitability. In fact, your competition seems to continuously corrode your profitability. Although your business has experimented with several sales-boosting strategies in the recent past, the top-line seems to remain stubbornly stuck. Typically because every time you win new customers, you also seem to lose existing ones at a similar pace. Long hours spent on cold calls, free consulting, brainstorming and endless discussions have not led to any improvements in the top-line.

Ineffective Marketing

In addition to conducting internal assessments and problem-solving initiatives, you may have also onboarded external consultants and marketing agencies. Guidance from friends and other industry colleagues may also have been sought. Almost without fail, all of these external advisors may have recommended to improve your 'lead generation' and marketing activities. And heeding their insights, you implemented a brand new CRM program, enhanced social media presence, embarked on email marketing and ensured your brand's presence at all relevant business events. However, despite these considerable enhancements in marketing and networking, there is still no significant growth for your business. What am I missing, you wonder.

Zero-Benefit It Upgrades

In recent years, your company has spent a small fortune to upgrade and improve your IT infrastructure, featuring new applications, larger technological frameworks as well as new gadgets to support the organization. These investments were supposed to create considerable efficiency that would contribute towards the bottom line. And it worked, for a while. After the initial few months of showing visible efficiency, your operational processes seem to have fallen back to old ways of doing things. While the IT infrastructure has provided you with faster processing powers, the manual processes, contextual and judgmental decision-making continue to exist. In the end, there is no measurable change in the overall efficiency of your organization.

Digital Challengers

Of late, many companies have been talking about the tremendous benefits digital transformation has delivered to their organizations. Many of them have referred to tools and techniques peers and competitors are deploying to service their customers. Many of these 'digitally-transformed' players are not even local, but are now successfully providing their goods and services through virtual platforms. And their transformation is not just about how they trade; thanks to the rich data that they now have access to, these digital players are able to articulate the needs of their customers much better. In fact, they seem to almost pre-empt challenges even before they occur! It is no surprise that these 'digital challengers' are winning new businesses at an unprecedented rate, while you are not.

Stop-Go Digital Innovation

Not that you are unaware of digital evolution or have not been inspired by these success stories. Motivated by some of these digital challengers in other industries and smartphone apps, your company also invested in a few digital innovations of its own. You had several design workshops, created in-depth conceptualization sessions and in some cases, you even went up to the POC stage. But not beyond that. Perhaps there was resistance from your internal leaders, who weren't very convinced about the need for and benefits of these digital innovations. Eventually, projects got shelved, the potential was not allowed to be nurtured, and you were bereft of any possible gain coming out of these innovations.

Checklist: Growth Inhibitors

1. Do you operate in a highly competitive market?
2. Do you operate in low innovation market?
3. Does your market segment have limited digital adoption?
4. Has your business growth been sluggish for at least 3 years?
5. Is there a certain level of frustration amongst your leadership team regarding their inability to grow your business?
6. Has there been a considerable amount of diverse initiatives

tried out in your organization to generate growth?

7. Has your organization been exposed to or are they exploring new-age digital technologies like cloud-computing, artificial intelligence, big data analytics, Internet-of-Things (IoT), Block-chain or Virtual Reality?

8. Has your organization earmarked a "digital-savvy" senior leadership (who is familiar with the technologies mentioned above) to lead innovation and market expansion?

9. Have you evaluated partnering with other companies to de-velop new products or services to create new revenue channels?

10. Has your company explored online revenue "supporting" opportunities including content marketing, digital sales funnels, high-volume social media management, online brand building?

11. Has your company invested in specialist skills to conduct big-data mining efforts?

12. Have you conducted "lateral thinking" innovation work-shops to generate ideas?

BUSINESS IN THE 2020S: THE 6 MAJOR TRENDS

As we enter the 2020s, we are going to witness unprecedented changes in the business world. Unfortunately, it has begun on a less-than-positive note with the COVID-19 crisis that is crippling world trade and economies in so many ways. Many businesses will be severely affected and may never be able to overcome it. On the other hand, digital technology has evolved rapidly over the past 10 years and we are going to witness its true power being unleashed during this decade, especially as a result of the pandemic.

Also in this decade, baby boomers — widely considered the loyalist generation — are set to retire from the active workforce in the coming decade. Simultaneously, much of the Gen-Z will join the work force.

All of these concurrent trends will have significant impacts on the world economy. For our purposes, I have identified six directions that I believe will play a defining role in the business world. All have a direct connection with digital technology.

- Baby Boomers and Gen-X approaching retirement
- COVID-19 defining a new normal
- Rapid technology advances
- Millennials' and Gen-Z's influence on work culture
- Shifts in cross-border commerce
- Deconstruction of jobs

Baby-Boomers And Gen-X Approaching Retirement

Most of the developed world is moving towards an ageing population, with the median age constantly moving higher. This includes countries in Western Europe, US, Japan and even China. This is because most baby-boomers will be 65 or older by 2030 and likely to retire in the coming decade if they have not already done so by now.

With advances in medicine and healthcare, people now will live longer than previous generations. When I was a child, I could not remember seeing a lot of people who were 90+ in age. Now, I see a lot more people in that population group.

This trend is bringing in some economic challenges for the individual countries. In general, older people need more medicines and access to healthcare systems. Therefore, we will see an increased dependency of this group on state funds, pensions and other financial subsidies related to healthcare systems. Secondly, as the age median moves up, there will be fewer people in the workforce to be able to support the government coffers and tax systems. These factors are going to strain the exchequers of most governments.

So, these governments would be desperately looking for answers to their problems. One of the area that they will look at would be digital and technology innovation. We are likely to witness a surge in Big Data analytics and artificial intelligence-based healthcare solutions. AI-based diagnostics, preventive health-care and robot-based monitoring are a few examples of developments in this space.

Covid-19 Defining A New Normal

The current pandemic has cast a long shadow over the global business ecosystem. Global supply-chains have been interrupted, physical interactions have been severely limited, and lockdowns have only allowed vital services to continue. How long this will last, the level of devastation this crisis will leave behind and when economies will bounce back, only time will tell.

We can, however, state with certainty that two distinct — and re-lated — phenomena will emerge.

First, we will have a 'New Normal' way of leading our lives just as we had after Hurricane Katrina, 9/11 and the SARS outbreak.

Second, we will witness an acceleration of digital adoption like never before. In fact, this one has already begun, and we will see a massive surge in the coming months. More transactions are going to be done online and through digital platforms. People would be averse to traveling soon, will prefer maintain social distancing and, in many instances, telecommute and work remotely. This will tremendously increase dependence on digital platforms.

Unfortunately, most businesses are woefully unprepared to adopt digital technologies swiftly. And even those who adopt them quickly are unable to unleash the exceptional opportun-ities because of faulty or uninformed adoption.

In most cases, there are companies that had adopted some levels of digital technology in their operations (albeit reluctantly), prior to the crisis. I say reluctantly because many in their leadership were nay-sayers and skeptics of digital technology. That is why, many of them did open digital channels but did not really focus on building it and exploiting its benefits. They chose instead to continue their focus on their main lines of business. Ironically, the current crisis has completely transformed their thinking and overnight 'shocked' them into becoming promoters of digital innovation.

But there are just a few of these lucky ones. Even for these companies, had they implemented digital the right way, they would be reaping the benefits of exceptional growth the way it is meant to be.

What most companies do not realize is that the digital medium not only provides an alternate medium to conduct business in, it also provides a massive number of spin-off opportunities that can be unleashed to generate exponential growth.

Like any other transformational change, every large-scale change needs a compelling reason to trigger the transformation. At many companies where the digital world was lurking as a low plan B option, the current crisis has just provided that massive compelling reason to transform and to adopt digital technology earnestly.

Rapid Technology Advances

We have witnessed unparalleled growth in technology in the past 10 years. This trend is only going to accelerate in the coming decade. We will increasingly witness technology entering spaces in ways that were unimaginable until recently.

For instance, in healthcare systems, Artificial Intelligence is going to be extensively used for diagnostics. In fact, we already see AI being used heavily in medical imaging and healthcare applications. These AI engines have far better accuracy than human beings in identifying and predicting illnesses such as cancer. AI is also going to be used for targeted marketing, inventory management, recruitment, and sophisticated business processes such as dynamic pricing.

Blockchain adoption as a multiparty system is going to gain traction, especially in the areas of supply chain and logistics. We are going to see more collaboration between multiple parties, consortiums and other associations being formed to reap benefits of using the multiparty system. Blockchain is going to tremendously raise transparency in a supply chain and thus, attack counter feeds and fraud problems with strong veracity.

We've all heard and read about the 5G technology being rolled out across the globe. When the power of 4G was combined with smartphones, it gave rise to the technological advances that we witnessed in the last decade. Uber, Airbnb, Netflix, and social media platforms, all benefitted from the power of 4G. Imagine the kind of innovation that 5G is likely to bring to our lives. From the usage of voice-based devices, autonomous driving to VR based apps, the power of 5G will be spectacular to experience.

Immersive media is yet another technology manifestation that is going to enter our lives much more prominently in this decade. VR, AR and 360° videos are going to be introduced in an affordable and usable manner. Be it conducting board meetings remotely, traveling to a virtual island for an experience or visually inspecting to lease an apartment, you will be using your smartphone equipped with 5G technology.

These are just a few examples from the massive spread of exciting things that are happening in the world of technology.

Millennials And Gen-Z Workforce

Most millennials are already in the workforce and Gen-Zs have just begun their professionals journeys as well. These two generations have grown up with technology. For many of them, it is difficult to comprehend the world before Google or Facebook.

This digitally-native generation is hardwired to think differently compared to baby boomers and Gen X. They use digital devices with the same alacrity as the previous generations used pen and paper. Taking photos and videos that was considered a novelty for the previous generation, has now been deeply integrated with the daily lives of this generation. Posting photos on Instagram or Facebook a few times in a day is quite common amongst this group. They are also very adept in searching for information online and using their social network to get answers for the challenges they may face.

As this group becomes a bigger part of the workforce, they will bring in their de facto digital thinking to their work.

Moreover, unlike prior generations that lived on loyalty, this generation is focused on experience. What this means for potential employers is that they must implement and adopt new sets of policies and guidelines that keep this group motivated and engaged in their work.

There is no question that this group — with its quintessential digital-influenced behaviors — is going to redefine our workplace and work culture.

Shifts In Cross-Border Commerce

Economic liberalization began in China in the late 70s and the country has been growing rapidly ever since to become the 2nd largest economy in the world and the de facto manufacturing hub for the planet. On the other side, the buying power of western economies remain strong and they continue to be beneficial trade partners for many economies. And the global trade diaspora is continuing to expand. Countries such as India, Brazil, South Africa, Turkey, Singapore, South Korea, and many others have joined the economic boom of liberalization in global trade. Over the past 30 years, globalization has grown into a powerful, omnipresent phenomenon.

As countries become larger economically, it is usually closely followed up by flexing political muscle power as well. Over the past few years, trade-related spats between China and the US have become a constant item on cable news networks. And now, the COVID-19 crisis exposed one of the ugly truths about the globalized world that we live in. The world has become over-dependent on Chinese manufacturing, and the current crisis has thrown up a huge barrage of challenges resulting from the mega supply-chain disruption.

As we readjust ourselves to the new normal, I believe most businesses would go back to their manufacturing base in China, but they would now also actively look to hedge their risks and certainly, explore alternate manufacturing hubs.

The disruption is not limited to just manufacturing or sourcing; free trade across the globe has meant that certain countries — especially in the emerging markets — have gained significantly, while on the other side, it has put considerable strains on the job markets in the more developed world. Countries such as India, Malaysia, Philippines, Mexico, Costa Rica, Romania, Poland, and Bulgaria have significantly benefitted from high-skilled, low cost professionals who could do the same jobs as their developed economy counterparts at a fraction of the cost.

This shift in the economic center-of-gravity that has taken place over the last 30 years, has now started showing up as discontent and unemployment issues in many countries. Political opportunists have taken advantage of the situation and have started raising nationalistic/ protectionist voices across the board. This would mean that the free flow that was taking place until the recent past may now increasingly come under nationalistic scrutiny and we could be seeing more trade barriers being put in place.

Fallout from the pandemic will only accelerate this current tension, and this will create significant trade issues as we start settling into the new normal.

Deconstruction Of Jobs

I kept this point as the last trend, because, as you can imagine, with all the changes taking place under the new normal along with rapid developments in the technology world, there would be huge impacts on job markets. Many of the jobs that we have known forever and have grown up with, are likely to disappear in the coming decade.

In the past, careers in accounting and finance were considered lucrative and hugely sought after. The first wave of impact happened with the introduction of computers. This was followed by massive outsourcing and offshoring that began in the 90s. And in the last decade, with the introduction of Robotics Process Automation (RPA), it has further eroded the value of these jobs. In the coming decade, we are likely to see more accounting and finance coordinators and managers rather than pure-play book-keepers. It is not that the need for accounting and finance will disappear, or that there will not be any jobs left in this space; it is simply that conventional job descriptions would go through massive upheavals soon.

Similarly, in the healthcare space, artificial intelligence, big data analytics, and immersive media would mean that machines would do a lot more diagnostics and analysis in the future. And human beings would be used primarily to monitor the process instead of operating it. With VR and AR, doctors and surgeons will be able to perform their discussions and even surgeries remotely. As you can see, this would mean that technicians who can operate these new applications and manage remote collaboration would be in much higher demand. On the other hand, jobs such as oncologists and other diagnostics-related roles are going to change dramatically.

With cost constraints and the rise of super specialized skills, most companies will not be able to afford and manage these resources in-house. And from a practical point of view, it would not even make sense if these resources are only required on a part-time basis. These conditions will give rise to the gig-economy with strong job marketplace platforms supporting them. We already see this shaping up through platforms like Upwork where companies can engage crowdsourced resources for specific skills that they want, without the necessity of employment and even the whole recruitment process.

Job deconstruction is going to redefine the way we live and work. And the train has already left the station.

◆ ◆ ◆

Checklist: Trends Impacting Your Business

This is a checklist to get a preliminary view on how business trends in 2020s are likely to impact your business.

- Was your organization adversely affected due to the COVID-19 crisis?
- Do you operate in a highly competitive and limited growth market?
- Do you have significant number of employees and other resources who work remotely?
- What is the aging population median of your organization?
- What is the demographic culture of your organization i.e. traditional, hierarchical, meritocratic, collaborative, etc.?
- Does your company have a written strategy that gets shared with employees?
- What is the relative importance given to digital initiatives in your company's strategy?
- Do you have people from millennial and/or Gen-Z groups in prominent leadership positions or being groomed as high-potential?
- Does your company conduct significant amount of cross-border business in terms of products and services?
- Does your business use artificial intelligence, big data analytics, Blockchain, AR/VR, IoT, smartphone-based apps or immersive media solutions?
- Does your company have experience in hiring and engaging free-lancers and consultants?
- Does your company engage consultants at senior levels or specialized skill levels?

IT IS NOT MY PROBLEM

One of the biggest threats in today's world is the lack of acknowledgement of the problem faced by businesses that need digital intervention. Be it a complete disregard of the looming competitive threats, disagreement on details of solution, missing ownership and accountability, or simply burying the head in the sand, the lack of acknowledgement may take various forms.

Companies that are planning a digital adoption in the future must comprehensively address the lack of acknowledgement. And this means not just recognizing the issues, but also taking firm and decisive actions. Most importantly, the organization should be strongly aligned and committed to a digital adoption initiative.

There Is No Problem

Many businesses believe that if they continue to operate the way they have done in the past, they will be fine. As these businesses continue to grow, they feel that there is no need to change the winning formula. Why would you want to disrupt something that is generating revenue at this stage? Sales guys are meeting their targets, operations is able to deliver continuously and the management is happy with the overall performance of the company. There is a level of contentment (read: complacence) that sets in. These businesses do not seem to notice that dark clouds are forming on the horizon. Look at what happened to Kodak. Once considered the gold standard of photography, Kodak did not notice how digital technology was going to alter the world. And the rest is history, quite literally for them.

The Problem Is Not Here

Whenever a problem occurs in a business, people tend to look for parties to blame. Sometimes they blame it on the system. One of the favorite fall guys would be the IT department in many companies. At other times, stagnant companies point towards market volatility. Some even blame their customers for not understanding the functionalities well enough. How many times have you heard of companies blaming themselves? In fact, by default, the finger never points at themselves to start with. Only when all other avenues get exhausted do people sometimes look at themselves for answers. Revenue growth, operational efficiencies and company performance are problematic apparently due to issues with somebody else or something else, never with the organization itself. And because the problem lies somewhere else, there seems to be no reason to deep-dive internally and evaluate digital adoption as an option.

The Problem Is Not Under My Control

Today's organizations are simply not designed to handle digital adoption the way it needs to be. The IT guy says that revenue generation is the job of sales and marketing. The marketing guys say digital innovation is the work of product development. The product guy says that new products — especially digital ones — should be decided by the strategy team. But the big question is, who owns it? Everybody and Nobody. And since nobody has digital adoption in their performance objectives, the problem to be solved is also not under their control. When a problem is not under the direct control of an existing team, they are unlikely to step up and own the problem and look for a solution. It is a lot easier to say instead: "The problem is not under my control."

I Have A Different Ideas

If you are facing issues with your sales performance, then why don't you get extra sales guys? If your advertising campaign is not yielding the results that you were looking for, maybe you need to raise the budget of your marketing effort. If customers are complaining about late deliveries, then perhaps the service delivery team needs to pull up their socks. Obviously, with a myopic view, all these problems seem to have different remedies. Even though most of us are quite familiar with the term root cause, people end up only looking at the symptoms and the visible causes. Unfortunately, most companies fail to notice the common root cause that can easily resolved if one were to explore digital technologies.

Not In Agreement With Details

Unless driven by a central team with an enterprise-wide authority, different teams would have their own unique requirement that needs specific technology. This can often be counter-intuitive, and the enterprise digital solution will not be aligned. A classic example is of implementation of chatbot solutions. Many companies have implemented chatbots and replaced their customer service people, but they forgot to put a team of data analysts who could mine the data and create powerful results. Other companies may have variations in level of awareness, biases or involvement, resulting in disagreements about the details of a solution.

Solution Has Negative Impact/ Fake News

Lack of proper training and skills often drive fear-mongering in organizations. Many technology adoptions have failed because people have blown the negative side of a solution out of proportion. What is worse that many of these negative stories are not even true. Whenever people are faced with transformation, most tend to push back. And this push back happens as they try to amplify the negative side and subdue the positive aspects. As an instance, non-crypto Blockchain implementations in the business world suffered serious setbacks as people started amplifying stories of multiple Ponzi schemes linked to crypto currencies. Many companies stopped their blockchain projects without even realizing that non-crypto Blockchain implementations have nothing to do with crypto currencies. But who is going to police this ignorance?

Who's Got The Money?

One of the most-used excuses that companies dish out is the lack of funds. I can understand that in the old days when companies would talk about computerization, ERP implementation and new product introductions, it used to need serious amounts of money, effort and would span a few years. But the world has radically changed since then. Most digital technology implementations happen within months if not weeks. Today, if one is planning a digital initiative as a multi-year project, there is definitely a serious flaw in the thinking. Moreover, with implementations in weeks and low-cost software, companies no longer need a war chest to fund their digital aspirations.

Lack Of Clarity

Conventional projects used to follow waterfall models with multi-year project plans. And it is expected that same models be followed in digital adoption as well. In any digital adoption exercises, there is high level of uncertainty at the initial stages. As you progress through the initiative, you start lifting the fog and discover key understanding that helps you define the next stages. Due to uncertainty and the habit of following conventional project management models, many organizations fail to go beyond the drawing board as team leaders expect upfront clarity about the details of the implementation. Case in point being the concept of a business case. Most companies still follow the practice that all transformation projects must be supported by a strong business case with clear ROIs (return on investment), financing requirements and benefits upfront. That is not how it works with digital transformation. Digital adoption requires multiple experiments do be conducted before you find the right fit for your business.

Risk-Averse Thinking

Some business leaders are hard-wired to be risk-takers whereas others are risk-averse. By definition, digital adoption will have a degree of uncertainty associated with it and thus, a certain element of risk. If your leadership team is largely composed of risk-averse individuals, you will struggle to get scaled digital adoption. Companies that are cost conscious or not very adventurous experimenting with new ideas, will have this issue a lot more and often than the ones that are open and continuously explore new ways of doing things when it comes to digital adoption.

It Is Your Problem

Companies must not look just at the symptoms and the surface causes. You must delve deep into your business. You have to identify and isolate each of the issues. And then characterize them from different angles so that you can address them comprehensively. Businesses across the globe are full of nay-sayers and risk averse people. Of course, they will be resistant to transformational change but that does not mean their concerns are not legitimate. You need to ensure that their voice also gets heard and their concerns handled. Only then, would you create the right environment for exploring digital technology and eventually lead to digital ideation and adoption. You have to take control because the problem, quite frankly, is yours.

Checklist: Reflection And Alignment Of Growth Problems

1. Is there a consensus that your organization is facing real growth challenges?
2. Does your leadership believe that your stunted growth is primarily a result of external market conditions?
3. Do you think that your leadership team is unable to come to a consensus on a cohesive growth strategy?
4. Is there bickering and high levels of discontent amongst your senior management team?
5. Does your IT team get blamed for most of your internal issues?
6. Do your sales and marketing team get blamed most for not being able to grow?
7. Do your executive leadership and senior management have a cohesive vision on how to create innovation and strategy for growth?

8. How often are strategic plans and outlooks revised during the year?

9. Do most of your functional and operational leaders stay within their boundaries of tasks and activities?

10. Have your IT, marketing, sales and operations team combined forces to collaborate and create new functions in the last 5 years?

11. Does your company have leaders that are well respected across your organization for their views and strategies?

THE PROCESS
OF IDEATION

Remember the first time in school when you were asked to write a sentence for a given word? At first, you were at a complete loss about the task. Then your teacher dropped a hint. It gave you some courage to think again and some ideas started forming. Then she gave an example. You quickly grasped the pattern and created a sentence based on it not straying too far away from the example your teacher had shared.

You must have seen the same pattern repeat in many instances during your educational and your professional life. Think of the time when your boss had asked you for suggestions for new initiatives. At the first instance, you may have felt awkward. But with practice, you became a pro.

Throughout your life, you must have had hundreds of such occasions where you were asked to offer some ideas. Unless somebody asked you to provide an idea for a NASA rocket fuel composition, I am pretty certain that you would have been able to give a few worthwhile suggestions.

However, you would have also encountered occasions where

your mind froze after a few ideas. It was then somebody like your teacher in school, your coach on the field, or your boss in the office gave some hints, contexts and examples that enabled you to come up with more ideas. They catalyzed the ideation process.

On the other side, remember the times when you desperately needed some ideas? You asked your team for some, but you ended up being appalled at the paucity or unoriginality of their thoughts. And lack of ideas meant that you could not make much progress in the direction that you wanted to.

In the digital world, companies desperately need to continually think up new and innovative ideas. Through these ideas, they can adopt digital technologies and create that buoyancy required for their growth acceleration.

Yet, we see many companies struggle at the kick-off itself — the process of generating fresh and unique ideas.

Over the years, I have conducted many ideation workshops across the globe. During my sessions, when I ask people for their ideas, initially most of them struggle. The moment I give them hints and tips, floodgates open and I get deluged by ideas. The idea catalysis begins.

Over the next few chapters, I will share various technics that I have used effectively to generate ideas. Each of these ideation technics give different perspectives and different ways to look at the process. Individually, each one of them have their own strengths and are applicable universally.

Here is a list of ideation technics:
- Orientation of Digital Adoption Framework
- Understanding customer types
- 100 DAF ideas using 6M+

Orientation Of Digital Adoption Framework

Based on 11 elements, this framework provides a 360 approach to digital adoption. Starting from User and Customer Experience, each box must be thought through, discussed and debated on what and how different aspects of digital techniques can be adopted in your business. This process is not based just on sales and marketing, or user experience; it delves into various channels and mediums that should be deployed and also looks at management and culture that demonstrate true digital capability. It also highlights the need to have digital operations and how to create a data organization, and eventually how to remodel infrastructure and IT management for the digital age.

Understanding Customer Types

Today, when people interact in the digital medium, they leave their digital footprint. When you visit a website, or when you click a link in an email, or when you conduct research or when you watch a video online, you are constantly leaving your mark in the digital world. These footprints are very valuable for businesses — they help them to understand you and your needs better. And by doing so, it gives the businesses opportunity to create targeted and bespoke solutions specifically for you.

We have categorized customers, prospects and users into 12 sets.

By reviewing these 12 sets and understanding perspectives unique to each of them, you will have plenty of things to think about.

100+ Ideas Based On 6M+

Some of you would be familiar with this technique and may have even used it in your work. But I believe most of you are not. Moreover, to give it a structure we have used the 6Ms (Man, Machine, Material, Method, Mother Nature, Measurement) and expanded it to include Communication, Organization, Leadership, Governance and Strategy in an ideation engine. The best way to use this matrix is create a set of 8-10 questions under each header to create a potentially 100-idea matrix.

DIGITAL ADOPTION FRAMEWORK

Most organizations incorrectly believe that digital adoption is a binary state, either you are a digital business, or you are not. In fact, many companies buy a digital solution for a peripheral function and start proclaiming that they are a digital company.

Unfortunately, digital adoption is a full transformation. Not only does it involve enabling technologies, it also means change in operations, in leadership, in thinking, in its proliferation across different function and finally, a transformed organization.

In the past, technology would help companies to conduct activities faster, cheaper, better, and more efficient. While the same continues even today but for a blue-blooded digital organization, it means a completely transformed way of conducting business.

Based on years of experience, and conducting extensive research on various frameworks and concepts, we have created a framework that we believe will help companies to break their digital aspirations into manageable chunks. Notable models that we drew our inspiration from included Digital Capability Model[1], Business Model Canvas[2] and The Value Chain[3] to create the Digital Adoption Framework.

Digital Adoption Framework

<table>
<tr><td colspan="3">User Experience</td><td colspan="2">Digital Operations</td></tr>
<tr><td rowspan="2">Digital Marketing</td><td>E-Commerce</td><td rowspan="2">Digital Interactions</td><td>Digital Management</td><td rowspan="2">Knowledge Marketing</td></tr>
<tr><td>Market Intelligence</td><td>Digital Culture</td></tr>
<tr><td colspan="2">Data Organization</td><td colspan="3">Infrastructure and Technology Management</td></tr>
</table>

Figure 3.1: Digital Adoption Framework

This framework is to create a digital adoption visualization for your organization. It has 11 functional areas where you can adopt digital and enabling technologies. This framework is a decisive canvas where you can articulate all areas where you can convert your business into a digital business and not just for only your products and services.

This aspect about digital business is essential to understand. Most of the businesses make a mistake thinking that by deploying a digital app, they can become a digital business. Whereas when you look at the canvas, you realize that there are so many different aspects that need to be considered and adopted before you can become a true digital company.

User Experience

This section covers whatever interaction you have with your customers. However, the strict definition of customers does not hold good anymore. There are people who use your products and services, there are non-customers who visit your website or comment on your social media post as well as there are those who are paying for your services and products. The entire group is now combined to new group called users. And any interaction with them on a digital platform will be covered under User eXperience or UX in short.

UX group would cover all users including your existing customers, potential buyers, enthusiasts, suppliers, alliance partners, media people or anybody who interacts with your company. By collecting data about your user's interaction, you can collect valuable insights about how your users and potential buyers are behaving and accordingly, you can tailor your marketing campaign.

In the past, companies would struggle to understand the behaviors of their potential buyers and others. Most of the available data was unstructured, and companies would have to depend on marketing research, customer surveys and independent analyst reports to gauge potential buyers. It was only when the person ended up buying your service or your product, that you started getting meaningful and structured information.

Another aspect that needs to be kept in mind is that in the digital world, it is no longer a single interaction. Thereby, experience is a collection of individual interactions that must be studied and converted to digital application.

Digital Operations

As a result of the current digital revolution, many companies would willingly and some reluctantly transform their physical companies into digital companies. In other cases, companies may diversify and create a separate and an independent business unit focusing only on digital technology.

These digital businesses will have enabling technologies as core to their operations. It can be in the form of a substantial online presence. It may have an online interface in form of a digital store for their physical goods. It may be selling wares through Facebook, Amazon, or other E-commerce platform. It may be using big-data analytics to generate insights. It can be artificial intelligence being used for diagnostics. Or it could use Blockchain as a multi-party consortium. In other words, there are diverse set of manifestations that a digital company may have. The critical element is to have an enabling technology as core to the business.

The first kind of digital operations would be those that are completely online businesses. Yellow pages setup their online platform in 2006 but it was only in January 2019 that they completely moved to the online world.

The second kind of businesses are those who have physical products or provide services in the physical world but their business sourcing and selling takes place through an E-commerce platform. It can be fashion brands, books, devices, gadget, and various other items. The key differentiator is that the business solely relies on selling through E-commerce platform. There is a burgeoning set of businesses that are thriving on selling products through Amazon, Bol.com, Zalando and other online platforms. Many of these businesses are broker businesses, and we now see an increase in the number of businesses that solely manufacture for E-commerce platforms.

The third kind of businesses are those which are using enabling technologies like big-data analytics, AI, IoT, Blockchain and VR/AR as their core. These businesses will be digitally native almost from the start. Healthcare diagnostics companies, market research firms, and even some service providers who will use digital technology as a core, will fall in this category.

Certain aspects of this section may have an overlap with other elements but keep in mind, that this section is relevant when a business has completely transformed itself into a digital business and shuts their previous business, or they have created an independent business unit to be digital.

Digital Marketing

Getting structured data systematically in the physical world, marketing campaigns have always been a challenge. However, as our interactions have increased in the digital world, so has the amount of digital footprint that we leave. These digital footprints provide rich information about your buyers as well as potential consumers. The data generated from these interactions can be systematically collected and analyzed for insights by companies.

One of the significant developments that has taken place in this space, is the introduction of digital marketing funnel. Some of you may be familiar with "AIDA" model in marketing. Though this model has existed for more than a hundred years, but with digital marketing AIDA model has shot into prominence.

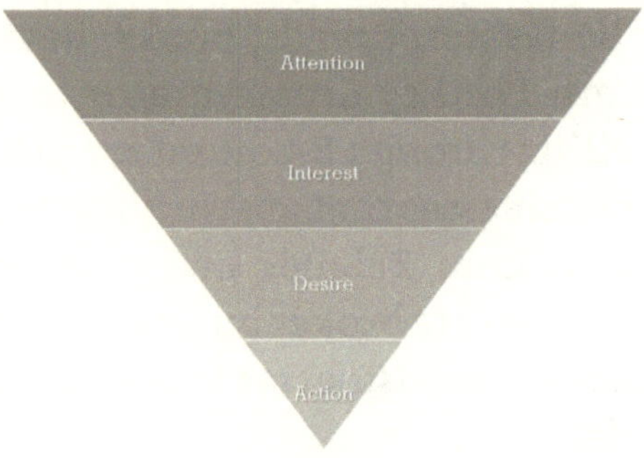

Figure 3.2: AIDA Digital Marketing Funnel

AIDA stands for Attention, Interest, Desire and Action. With so much of interaction taking place in the digital space, companies can design and develop specific components for each stage. The aim of the AIDA model is to take a potential customer through the complete experience journey starting from the awareness stage till the actual purchase.

Attention

Once a strategic campaign has been decided and signed off by the leadership, this is where the digital marketing funnel starts. In this stage, you would ask the following questions:
- Who is your target group or groups? *User profiling*
- What are some of the problems and challenges faced by

your target group? *Empathy mapping*

\- What kind of solutions is your target group looking for? *Market intelligence*

\- How can your solution potentially help your target group? *Product-market fit*

In addition, you need to conduct research on the following:

\- How is the target group articulating their challenges and pains? Social media chatter, industry report, 3rd party surveys, sales team's feedback, etc.

\- How are they expecting to find a solution? Are they contacting consultants, attending seminars on this topic, surfing specific websites?

\- How are you planning to create awareness and seek their attention? What channels would you use? What messaging and copyrighting will you need to do?

Depending on the answers to the above questions, you will design your marketing campaign. Depending on the channel, you will start creating content for the same. Obviously, different channels would mean different approaches. An Instagram may need a visual story, a twitter would need punch one-liners or product offers, and your email will need a grabbing headline.

Interest

Once you have created an attention in the market, and you find that your target group is showing interest, you must figure out how to maintain that interest.

And how do you figure out that your initial awareness campaign has generated an interest? Through clicks, time-spent, opens, etc.

For them to maintain their interest, your company shares some in-depth blogs, articles or throws in initial hooks in the form of offering them some freebies if they continue to be a part of your target group's journey.

Desire

Some businesses can not differentiate between these 2 steps: interest and desire. Interest is where your target group is curious to learn more about your products or your services. Desire is where your target group is convinced about your product and services being a potential solution for your problems. They are now evaluating other aspects including affordability, validation, market feedback, any negative reviews as well as repeat inspection.

Increase in the number of opens of the same emails, increased visit frequency to your website, potential interaction with your chatbots and maybe customer service all signifies an increase in the desirability of your target group.

Action

This is the last stage of the funnel where your target group buys your product or your services. You must be careful about putting noticeably clear Call-to-Actions (CTAs) at this stage so that your potential buyer can smoothly transition from being a prospect to an actual buyer.

There is a delicate approach required for this stage. You need to position your CTAs very strategically on your webpage or other medium. You do not want to appear over-zealous and on the other side, you do not want to lose your potential buyer since the person could not find the CTA button.

With digital marketing campaign, you now have an opportunity to guide your target group in a structured way to buy your products and services. And this structured approach can hugely increase your conversion rate as well as your revenue line.

E-Commerce

For many companies that deal with physical products, digital technologies can offer them virtual marketplaces that they can use to sell their products. This is however, not restricted to physical products only. You can use platforms like Udemy, Coursera and others to sell your digital training products. You can sell your own eBooks on Amazon or Nooks. You can even use affiliate marketing technics to sell your products on a 3rd party platform.

These virtual marketplaces primarily come in two flavors. The first flavor is where you use your own platform. You can sell your trainings, diagnostics, eBooks, software, application, cloud-solutions on your own platform or platforms that give you dedicated cloud space. Platforms like Thinkific or Teachable would provide platforms where you can sell your online training. The cloud space and web pages are dedicated to your business only. Whether you have a single product or a complete portfolio, you have a dedicated web link. This is highly suitable for businesses that have a range of products in their portfolio, and it is good for your brand building. Essentially, these platforms are giving you enabling tools to fast track your digital adoption. Both Thinkific and Teachable provide pre-defined templates to create online courses so make it dramatically easy for businesses to create a professional looking online training platform.

The second flavor is 3rd party platforms like Amazon, eBay, Airbnb, Upwork when the actual digital marketplace is owned by a 3rd party. This is suitable for businesses that want a digital platform for their physical products. It can be fashion, retail, books, or even spare capacity in your house, or you want to solicit freelance work for your specialist skills, these e-commerce platforms have come a long way. Platforms like Amazon and eBay are multi-product platforms where you can sell your gadgets, but you can sell books as well. This can be attractive for broker businesses who can source products from physical markets and sell them through these platforms. Platforms like Airbnb and Upwork are specialized marketplaces. Airbnb would sell spare capacity rooms for short-term rental whereas Upwork is a digital marketplace for skills.

Depending on the nature of your business and the kind of market access you are looking for you can decide what is more relevant for your business. Moreover, it is not an either-or choice. Many businesses choose both the options. As a publisher, you may decide to sell your books through multiple channels. A fashion brand may have their own channels, but they can also, sell through 3rd party channels. In fact, most of the fashion houses choose both the options.

At the end, if you can get benefitted from being on multiple platforms, then that is the approach you need to take. However, if it dilutes your brand value, you may decide to stay with your own platform.

Market Intelligence

There are huge amounts of data that is available in the public domains. This is the element where you use specialized skills to gather data both structured and unstructured from the market, from third-party databases, research journals, educational institutes, and feedback from your customers, suppliers, and partners. You harness the data to extract useful information and knowledge that can be leveraged to create a competitive edge for you.

There are multiple ways this available data can be used. Here are five uses under this category that I believe you will find useful.

Potential clients

By scouring through large swathes of data, you can get a deep understanding about the market. You can obtain powerful insights through UX research and digital marketing. This can be a great source of potential clients for you.

Competitive edge

By studying and distilling information from public domains,

you get a far better comprehension about your market. How are your competitors faring, what are the new trends in the market, what are some of the potential challenges, who is disrupting your market and most importantly, what products are performing well and at what price points, are just a few strategic questions that can get addressed by market intelligence. You can recreate your customer segmentation, create specific pricing and discounts by segments, as well as look at product diversification by understanding the dynamics of the market.

Whitepaper

By analyzing data, you can create your own market intelligence. This market intelligence can then be used to create whitepaper, blogs, and other insights that you can share online. This can be used as a lead-magnet for your business

Research-as-a-service

Companies that have a strong base in a certain industry and have access to a team of analysts, can easily create research-as-a-service as a potential product. While there are huge amounts of information available on the world wide web, most of it is unstructured and there is a genuine paucity of quality insights. Having a strong base in a certain industry, can give you an edge to create value-added research-as-a-service for your business.

Partnerships, alliances, and M&A

By understanding the market dynamics, you will also, recognize the players that operate in your existing market as well as new one. You can use this information to identify potential partners and alliances to access new markets or consolidate your position in the existing market. You can even explore possibilities of creating joint-ventures and in some, cases pursue an acquisition or investment strategy as well. This form of market intelligence is extensively used by strategic business buyers, private equities, and institutional investors.

Overall, market intelligence as a category had limited power prior to the internet revolution. And now, it can be a formidable tool for any business irrespective of their size or location.

Digital Interactions

This element covers all the channels, platforms and media being used to interact with your users, potential buyers, and customers. Some users use a single medium to interact with a business, others use several channels, and in some cases, an average user interchangeably uses different channels at different points in time.

In the past you only had a limited number of ways that you could interact. You could use land mail, fax, email, phone calls and physical meetings. But now in the digital medium there are hundreds of different options and channels that you can choose from.

You can use MailChimp to send out emails to your subscribers, you may use YouTube to share videos, you may use LinkedIn for professional digital advertisements, you may use simple emails for business transactions, you may leave comments on the website and various other methods.

To keep a track of different channels and their effectiveness, you need understand the dynamics of each of these channels. This will not only allow you to connect with your users through different mediums but will also tell you which channels are more effective in comparison to others. An example that I can share from our own experience is when we advertise with LinkedIn versus Facebook. With LinkedIn, we tend to get more professional interactions whereas Facebook provides the fun element.

We have divided these interactions in the following categories:

Social media

It includes platforms like Facebook, Instagram, LinkedIn, Twitter, and the others. Your users interact with your company pages on these platforms, or follow key people of your leadership team, or the same could be on your events page or a showcase page.

Usually, users will use these platforms to provide feedback or voice opinions. In some cases, they will complain about your product or services. In other cases, they might post positive comments about you.

Most importantly, through social media you can create a fanbase, a community of users who like your company as well as a collaboration channel between you and your users.

Moreover, from the interactions you have, you will be able to gauge the levels of interest of your users in your posts based on likes, shares, and comments

Content platforms

Content platforms like YouTube, Podcasts, SlideShare and blog sites let you post audios, videos and blogs related to your business, your products, and services. You can post informational material, opinions, market intelligence as well as promotional material on these platforms. These platforms can provide great avenues to share your experience, knowledge, and expertise with rest of the world.

E-Commerce platforms

This sub-category covers platforms like Amazon, and others that you use to display, share, and/or sell your products. This is a platform where users leave comments, providing you with a great source of feedback about your products and services.

Web traffic

Traffic that flows to your website in another form of interaction with your users. From the volume, you can discern the condition of your website. By studying their behavior while interacting with your website can give you profound insights. You can easily figure out; what pages attract your users and what do not. The most important thing is that Google has its algorithm based on user interaction with your platform, for ranking your page during a search process

Email

You now have the option of keeping in touch with your users through individual emails sent from your own mailbox or it can be through mass broadcasts and newsletters sent through a 3rd-party like Mailchimp and Mailer lite. If your business has hundreds of users, it may be difficult to keep sending them individually crafted emails. There is a time and place where you will need to send those ones as well. However, when you need to send bulk emails, platforms like Mailchimp make a huge difference. You can analyze how many emails were opened, how many people clicked on links in your email, how many people shared your email, etc. At the same time, if people are no longer interested, they can also choose to unsubscribe to your email broadcasts. This can be a cumbersome process if you had to update the status of these users manually in your CRM or lead database. However, with in-built functionalities, these platforms get these administrations done automatically.

Survey platforms

Survey platforms like SurveyMonkey and Typeforms are great

tools to collect information from your users and independent people about your business, product, as well as market research information. Many businesses regularly keep in touch with engaging their users through surveys and focus groups especially before they launch a new product or a new campaign.

Many businesses overlook the power of using surveys to interact with their customers and users in a non-intrusive way.

Businesses may choose one medium versus the other, or a combination but they should remember that it is no longer sufficient to treat each of these channels independently but they should be treated as part of a cohesive, coordinated set. When you run a campaign now, you need to run it as a single campaign with an omni-channel perspective. An average user toggles between different channels during the same campaign. A user may read your email from their smartphones which was sent from MailChimp, reply to the email that goes to your own mailbox, download the freebie from their desktop and then share the news about the freebie on Facebook.

Another important aspect of an omni-channel is to ensure that the campaign is seen by your target group. With so much of information being shared, and so many emails ending up in junk folders, it is quite possible that the emails are either missed out, not seen or not actioned upon by your users before they move on to the next item. That is why, it is important that other channels can re-enforce the visibility of your campaigns.

Digital Management

To run an organization, you need a full-fledged management system and leadership team. Similarly, to run a digital program or a digital business, you need a similar construct. You will need Digital savvy leadership, specialized skills, change management as well as governance mechanisms, performance measurements, project management office and various other components including policies and guidelines to make it an effective digital organization.

Digital savvy leadership

Many businesses that struggle with digital adoption is primarily due to their executive leadership team's lack of understanding of the power of these enabling technologies. On the other side, companies that have digitally savvy CEO or COO have been extremely successful in making that transition. CXOs who understand the power of social interactions through online platforms or understand how market intelligence can be effectively used to gather strong insights are likely to develop better understanding about their users and consumers. Similarly, executives who understand the power of AI or are using IoT in their business, can creatively develop a portfolio of products.

Digitally savvy does not mean that they need to know how to write codes in these platforms. It means that they have a good understanding of how these enabling technologies can be effectively adopted for their businesses and how they can help their organizations grow.

Specialized skills

Adoption of digital technologies does not mean you need to hire dozens of data scientists or AI engineers. It means that you need a work force that is adept in working with digital marketing funnels, social media, content marketing and several other aspects. In some cases, you may need to hire super specialists and quants, but it is also possible that you may acquire these services from a 3rd party on a pay-as-you-go service or partner with them for digital co-creation.

Change management

As your organization transforms into a digital organization, you need to focus on the requirements of change management. This can mean communication at different points of transition, but this can also mean counselling through the job deconstruction process

Governance

Your digital organization will need its own governance mechanism, management as well as clearly defined performance measurements. This will help you achieve your digital adoption objectives easily but also, provide you with the mechanism to manage daily operations.

Policies and procedures

Many of your organizational policies and procedures will no longer be valid or be relevant once your digital adoption process is completed. Your company will need to revamp your policies and procedures. This could be related to the usage of digital media, online presence but also, restrictions and information security related to your company information.

Digital Culture

To ensure that your organization gets truly digital, you will need to ensure that your organization culture also reflects that. Without the necessary thinking, openness, eagerness to learn and continuously improve, your organization will always have a chance of going back to old ways of doing things. No matter how exciting the digital technologies may sound, habits have a way of creeping back into our lives if we do not address them properly.

Rapid Innovation

First and foremost, required for a digital organization is to have rapid innovation. This is to ensure that there is no procrastination happening once a round of innovations are conducted. Secondly, it creates a buzz amongst the teams that ensures further engagement, motivation and most important, brings new ideas that can create business growth.

Fail fast, learn faster

Rapid innovation would also, mean that many experiments would fail. Instead of getting into a blame game, a digital organization should have guidelines and frameworks in place that foster quick analysis and learning from the experiment so that those faults can be avoided in further experiments.

Experiment in volume

One can truly extract good insights when experiments are conducted in volume. They will ensure deeper understanding of the market and user behavior. It will also prevent from getting any parallax views which may result in distorted understanding.

Enabling tools

To conduct experiments and innovation, teams need to be given right tools, templates, software. With the plethora of open and free software, companies have a lot of options to choose from. However, for consistency and standardization, care must be taken, and consensus driven in the organization on what preferred tools and software to use. If you plan to use a tool, use Eventbrite as a tool to attract people but use Mailchimp as your CRM. Also, do not have some of your team members storing information in Eventbrite and the others in Mailchimp to avoid confusion.

Training

New digital platforms as well as software tools would need adequate training for the workforce. In addition, there need to be regular refreshers for the team to keep them updated. Apart from that, teams also need to ensure entire organizations get trained in new applications.

Mentoring

During the transformation stage and the new digital organization, there will be a constant need for supervising, coaching, and mentoring the larger teams. You will need to think of change agents, champions and group coaches who can help, support and mentor organizations in digital adoption.

Digital culture is an important foundational element to create a sustainable organization. The change in culture needs to be driven with the right ingredients and elements.

Knowledge Management

Every organization sits on top of a mountain of unearthed value. Most of them do not realize the importance or do not have the capability of unlocking the potential from this mountain of value.

The extraction and distribution of these experiential values to drive growth and effectiveness of an organization is termed as knowledge management. To use these bites of knowledge in marketing would be referred to as knowledge marketing.

While knowledge management is important for all businesses, it can be of immense value for human centric or knowledge centric organizations.

In the digital era that we live in, it is no longer enough to just talk about features of your products and services. In fact, due to digital access many businesses are struggling to maintain their differentiator. Let us look at consulting business. No matter what your services are, there will be hundreds if not thousands who will appear to give the same services, bring the same benefits and saying the same thing about their services.

On the other hand, the businesses who share their tools, technics, templates, case studies and experiences through whitepapers, blogs, videos, and other channels get better quality leads and higher conversion rate.

Knowledge marketing becomes a key differentiating tool for any digital business. The reasons are described below.

Credibility

The moment you create a whitepaper, publish a blog, and put a video online, it establishes you as an instant authority of your subject. People believe that if you have put something in the public domain then you must be credible.

Relevance

Many businesses may struggle to adopt any change. This problem gets compounded when the technology landscape is rapidly changing around them. Businesses may understand the power of an enabling technology but if they cannot create relevance, they cannot conceptualize a solution for their own business. I remember a conversation a few years back. I was speaking with an executive leader of a large multinational corporation on the benefits of Blockchain. While the person understood the functionalities of Blockchain, he was struggling to conceptualize on how to apply it to his organization. I had to help him walk through a couple of scenarios before he clearly understood the relevance and thus the benefit of the technology.

Many people would study and understand the functionalities of new technologies but without comprehension on how to apply it, they would stay on the fence.

Pull marketing

Best part of knowledge marketing is that it is a pull-marketing. As you establish credibility and relevance of digital technology, you will find that potential clients come to you more than your need to go to them. The credibility also, reduces the need for extensive convincing that is usually required through other means. Moreover, it gives you an edge to charge premium pricing for your services.

Fear of IP

Many companies are afraid of adopting knowledge marketing. Quite commonly I hear this argument from companies, that if they share their experience, their IP will become public and maybe adopted by their competitors.

"KEEPING KNOWLEDGE ERODES POWER. SHARING IS THE FUEL TO YOUR GROWTH ENGINE." - UNKNOWN

There are five things I would like to say in support of this:
-   One is that if it were so easy then every business would become super profitable businesses by reading books.
-   Second, your experience and expertise can never be taken away from you. It also, never reduces. It only grows.
-   By not letting your experience being shared, you are only restricting your business from growing.
-   If you have thought about it, there must be hundred others who have thought about it as well. So, you are not unique and you, are not the only one that can solve the problem
-   There is always a place to protect your IP (like a secret sauce). But it should not be confused experience.

By effectively marketing your knowledge, you can create a robust knowledge management organization. Knowledge marketing can tremendously increase your visibility in the market, lend massive credibility and the best part is that customers come to you rather than you chase them and pay a premium fee.

Data Organization

The era prior to digital adoption, we would talk about supply-chain, logistics, manufacturing, assembly-lines, and operations. With digital adoption and gargantuan amounts of data being generated, we would see similar structures being positioned to manage data. This new setup is going to be called data organization.

Data organization will be at the confluence of digital technology and conventional management structures. Governance, strategy, performance measurement, information flow, data economics as well as data sovereignty will need to be revamped.

Data ownership

One of the biggest questions soon, will be around ownership of data. With increased awareness around data privacy and regulations being implemented, organizations need to review what data can be owned by them vs not.

Every time I get a call from my bank, my bank asks me about my date of birth as well as specific items like my home address. What if I do not feel comfortable with sharing this information with a 3rd party like a bank.

If we look at another example, your impression would be quite different. Suppose you had a pain in your abdomen, and you had to visit a doctor. The doctor would ask you a few questions and make a diagnostic assessment. This is where it gets interesting. As the pain was yours, is it your data to own? What would be able to do with the data without the intervention of a doctor. Is doctor the owner of the diagnostic result data?

Data is the new gold. Questions like the ones above will be asked more often. In the future, these voices will only get pronounced and amplified.

Digital assembly line

Like in the physical world, raw material goes through an assembly line before it converts into a finished product. Similarly, in digital organizations, flow of data will also follow a similar path. And as with the physical structure, digital structure will also have different teams with different value-creation, deliverables, and accountability.

Digital waste

Huge amounts of data are being generated every second. With further advances in technology, the data management problem is only going to get bigger. And one of the big issues is going to be around digital waste.

Most organizations will not pay heed to this as digital storage devices get cheaper. However, the problem is likely to arise in the form of disposal, archival and retrieval.

Look at the care that you take disposing physical letters. How many of us, can say the same thing about your e-mails? Millions of documents get created before we can bat an eyelid. You may have taken measures to protect your data on your desktop. But how about all the social media posts, all the documents that you have shared in the cyber-space and all the transactions that you were involved in, but are not actively aware? Information about you that is stored by your bank, by your credit card provider, by the loyalty program cards and many other places. As you know only too well, many cyberattacks take place randomly, and companies lose valuable customer information.

Data organization is no longer a nice to have, it is time that organizations start reviewing this seriously.

Infrastructure Management

This is the element of DAF. To support everything that is required from a technology perspective to make your company digital is covered under this element. What applications to use, what sort of storage facilities, cloud computing, software licenses and hardware required to run a digital organization, are all included in this element.

Scaling flexibility

In a digital business, there is a going to be an increased need of flexibility in scaling up and scaling down as per the need of the organization. When a new system gets implemented, organizations may need to scale-up their environments to cater for testing and development. During a stable operations period, this requirement becomes redundant.

Now, with Google, Microsoft, and Amazon, all trying to woo customers to get to their platform, interoperability will need to be reviewed carefully as well.

Cyber and information security

Much of the information that is in the public cloud has a lot of security and protection these days. However, the challenge is with millions of freebie apps that are being used, it is the unstructured data that is constantly being downloaded to your devices and suspicious website visits that make your system more prone to cyberattacks.

A sinister side of information security is going to be doctored data and fake news. With information being shared so openly, in such quick time especially in case of sensational news, organizations will be faced with double problems. One is the information security itself and the other one, will be damage control.

Infrastructure organization

Infrastructure management in the digital world needs to be thought through again. In the past, organizations needed to maintain specialized skills within their own organizations, to manage expensive hardware and software. Now, with much of physical infrastructure being replaced by cloud-computing, we will need different kinds of skills in our organization. Rather than maintaining specialized skills, we will need people who are good at problem solving and collaborating with other people include remote teams as well as support teams of the service provider.

In the future, business continuity and disaster recovery plans, will get replaced with digital twins' model. This again, would need different skills than the past.

Finally, any specialized software and tools like IoT, AI, robotics, and managing digital funnels will all need a new set of skills.

Organizations will need to think of reskilling their own staff as well as get used to the idea of gig economy, where it hires people on short-term contracts or even part time rather than full-time employees.

Summary

These were the 11 items that make the Digital Adoption Framework (DAF). DAF is meant to provide a structure by which a company can convert its organizational digital adoption strategy to specific operational level visualization.

By discussing this framework with your team, you should be able to generate a huge number of ideas from which you should easily be able to short-list and prioritize the ideas that you can further develop.

Using this framework, you can start building your story and create a detailed strategy based on solid foundational blocks. With the framework, you should be confidently able to embark on a digital adoption journey.

Whether you are going to completely become a digital business, a physical business with a digital front-end or simply adopt few digital elements will depend on the individual needs of your organization. As mentioned earlier, whether we like it or not, like in the 90s where most companies moved their information to servers and computers, similarly, in this digital age, all companies irrespective of what business they are in, will move to become technology companies.

◆ ◆ ◆

Checklist: Baselining For Digital Adoption

This is a checklist that you should use before you start using DAF.

1. What is the compelling reason that is driving your organization to become digital?

2. Do you have digital expertise in your executive and senior management team?

3. Is there a separate digital strategy of your organization?

4. Has your organization run transformational projects in the last 5-7 years like ERP implementation, or any other project that impacted the entire organization and which needed significant involvement of people in various parts of the organization?

5. How would you describe your business's social media presence? What is the primary use of the social media presence?

6. Does your organization run digital marketing campaigns?

7. What are the different digital channels that your company uses to interact with its customers?

8. How does your company create awareness about your products, services, capabilities and experience with non-customers, and other users?

9. Does your company publish white-papers, articles, blogs,

and videos consistently, or is it ad hoc in nature?

10.   Do you have a digital team led by a chief digital officer or is it handled by your IT team?

11.   Is your organization using any of the latest enabling technologies in main functions (not peripheral) including IoT, AI, Big data analytics, Blockchain and/or VR/AR?

12.   What 11 elements is your company likely to adopt?

13.   Which of the 11 elements is your company likely to avoid and why?

14.   Is your organization experienced in engaging highly skilled and expensive external resources?

15.   In your opinion, if your organization did not adopt digital technology in the next 5 years, what do you foresee is going to be the future of your company?

16.   Do you think your current job will exist in 5 years time?

Notes:

1. Jace An, 77 Building Blocks of Digital Transformation, written by a digital practitioner, Story Tree FDC, 2019

2. Alexander Osterwalder and Yves Pigneur, Business Model Generation: A Handbook for Visionaries, Game Changers, and Challengers, John Wiley & Sons, Inc., 2010

3. Michael E. Porter, Competitive Advantage: Creating and Sustaining Superior Performance, Free Press, 1985

THE CUSTOMER IS WHO?

Conventional definitions of 'customer' have a simplistic view of all who consume your products or services. The fact is that there is no one single kind of customer; traditional definitions are not broad enough to cover all the individual groups that interact with your company. In the past, it was quite easy to describe somebody as a customer who purchases something from your company and pays a certain amount of money for the purchase. In the digital world, the concept of purchase has been completely redefined. Now, anybody who gives something of value to your business can be a customer. But this value may not be in direct monetary terms. That is why, many companies refer to them as users instead of customers.

Digital technology has created this ability for companies to break down all prospects or non-customer groups into several categories based on their needs and levels of interaction. In the conventional business world, all the people who show interest in your product but have not yet bought them, are usually clubbed together to form the lead or prospect group. Through digital marketing and online interactions, you can get huge amounts of data that can help you segment this big prospect group further into multiple, distinct categories, depending on their past and current behaviors.

The other aspect that we need to understands about modern customer behavior is that it is no longer enough to fulfill their functional requirements. Consumers and users now give much higher importance to the entire experience or the journey rather than the specific action of fulfilment. By understanding the emotional and aspirational aspects about your customers, you can significantly boost customer loyalty and offer them bespoke solutions that are specific, relevant and tailored to their needs and expectations.

Customer Profiling

Let us first start with understanding different types of customers. In this section, we have expanded the definition of customers to include users, prospects, unaware customers, ex-customers and existing customers as well via 12 categories.

The regulars

This is the easiest group to understand. These people are your existing, paying customers. If you are in the consumer business, these people are regular buyers of your services and goods. From the frequency of usage and their customer profiles, you can ascertain their buying patterns. You can also gather information about their likes and dislikes through customer surveys and interviews. And in case of B2B transactions, you can almost determine the pattern that is likely to be followed at the time of purchase. The people in this group possibly have customer loyalty cards or have long-term contracts with your business.

The loyalists

This one is an extension of the first group of existing or regular customers. The difference being that not only do they buy from you actively, they are also extremely loyal to your business. They will always come to you for the same service and products that others may offer even at a discount. These loyal customers are also likely to influence their friends and network, and promote your business to them through word-of-mouth.

The once-upon-a-timers

These are customers who have bought your products or services in the past, but have not repeated that behavior over the last year or two. There can be various reasons as to why they no longer buy from you. They may not need your services and products any longer, or they might have found alternatives. But in general, they never expressed any displeasure with your products, not did they swear loyalty to your company.

The defectors

This segment of customers defected to your competitor either on their own or were poached by your rivals. Interestingly, what has been observed is that after the initial euphoria of defection has waned, many customers state that the changeover did not result in a more satisfactory buying experience — they felt the same level of indifferent support from their new supplier that they did from your business. From the customer's point of view, the reasons for defecting were defeated and they ended up disillusioned and frustrated.

Annoyed exes

Every business has customers who leave them due to unsatisfied levels of quality or services. Most of the time, they leave as a knee-jerk response to a specific annoying transaction rather than a strategic reason. On delving deeper, one can see that the customers tried to raise a flag on the issue with your business, but their complaints were either never heard or were not acted upon. This apathetic approach is the biggest reason for customers leaving due to an issue of quality. Poor customer service made an already difficult situation irreversibly worse.

Unhappy customers

These are the existing set of customers who have expressed frustration or unhappiness about your services or products. The complaints could be over quality, service or experience issues, and they would have voiced their displeasure to somebody in your organization. This somebody could be a customer service rep, service delivery personnel or perhaps even a manager-level employee. Unless this somebody is part of a service desk, chances are that the unhappy voices are never recorded in a system anywhere in your organization. And if left unaddressed, it can corrode the level of their loyalty and ultimately lead to defection.

Non-paying customers

Now this is a rather interesting category. Your business needs them to function, but they never pay anything to you. This group is very prominent in digital businesses and are referred to as users instead of customers. This group would include customers who do not spend any money on you (who are part of a free trial), users (who only are interested in free, limited functionality products), subscribers (who have subscribed to your newsletters, free webinars) and followers (on social media platforms like LinkedIn, Facebook and Instagram). All these people need to be accorded many features that are similar to your paying customers. They may not have a conventional contract with you, but you would normally ask them to sign off on a T&C with your company on your digital platforms.

The next few sub-categories are an extension of this group — individuals who have never bought from you.

On-the-fence users

There are individuals who have expressed interest in your products and services several times, but never end up purchasing them. They may find your product valuable, but perhaps the price-tag is out of reach. Or, they may be fine with your price-tag, but do not want to pay the entire amount in one go, preferring a monthly payout instead. It is also possible that they find your product to be the best fit for their need, but their needs are not completely fulfilled by your own product alone; they may need to supplement it with other items. This group can also be influenced by word-of-mouth or user reviews.

Research majors

There are users who have recently initiated their search for solutions. They conduct online searches, read up books and publications, connect with experts, watch videos, and listen to podcasts to raise their understanding of various solutions. During this research journey, they start defining their own acceptance criteria for a solution that will be relevant and work for them. Typically, they will tend to have definite views on product and experience quality and can be quite demanding.

Unaware potentials

These are businesses and individuals who fit your customer profile perfectly. They have specific requirements that can be fulfilled by your products and services. And they will pay a fee which is in your sweet spot. Unfortunately, they do not know you. They are completely unaware of your existence.

Chain customers

These are customers of businesses that operate downstream or upstream from your business. Many of these customers have requirements that can be fulfilled by your own products and services, which can be bundled together with your downstream/upstream partner or can sold independently to this customer group. These customers may also have unrecognized/ unexpressed or implicit needs that have not been crystalized yet.

Latent customers

The last sub-set of non-paying customers comprise those individuals or businesses you have not yet 'poked' to acknowledge a need for your solutions and services. Either they are unaware of their problems (and therefore, the need for a service or solution), or addressing those issues is not a priority for them at this time. In any case, without expert help they may not even acknowledge the need until they hit a disaster tipping point.

Checklist: Different Faces Of Your Customer

1. Do you have all your users and customers mapped in the segments mentioned in this chapter or in a similar framework?
2. Does each segment have a different sales and marketing strategy?

3. Are you clear with your marketing messaging and value proposition for different classes of customers?
4. Do you have customer journey mapping laid out and documented?
5. Do you have an user journey (unaware-suspect-prospect-convert) mapped out and documented?
6. Do you have additional interactions with your customers and users that go beyond sharing of features and benefits of your products and services?
7. How often do your customers talk about you, with their peers and clients?
8. What is your strategy to create mass awareness about the specific problems your company's products and services can solve (rather than the features and benefits)?
9. How often do you conduct training and workshops with different user groups to increase awareness?
10. Do your potential buyers constantly make unyielding demands?
11. What do you think is the relative size of your existing base compared to all other types of users and customers mentioned in this chapter?
12. If you were to win 10% of the total business from the group of non-customers identified in the chapter, how much growth will it give you?

CUSTOMER PROFILE-BASED IDEATION

Whenever an organization needs to think of a new strategy, it is always advisable to start with your customer. While most products and services provide functional benefits to their clients, they almost always fall short on emotional and aspirational aspects. It is not surprising to see that people can only recollect a handful of products and services that they were wow-ed with.

Going beyond customers' needs, wants, aspirations, motivations, operating rigor, their method of engagements, their job requirements as well as their own personal background can offer a unique perspective about them. By studying their needs and analyzing their behavior, you will be able to unearth a number of opportunities to wow your customers and grow your business. In these opportunities, you will also come across requirements that you will help in your digital ideation.

Customer Characterization

In this chapter, we introduce you to customer profile framework.

Our framework leverages elements of customer profiling and customer empathy to provide a comprehensive understanding of your customer and their behavior. The customer profile framework can be used universally when describing an individual. This can be an existing customer relationship person, an influencer in your client's company or a decision maker. The framework should also be used to capture details about prospects and individuals who have initiated interest in the topic.

You should use the framework to create a set of questions to ask your customers. By using a bit of critical thinking, you can easily enrich the question database. Use the set of questions through a formal interview process or in an informal interaction. You may decide to spread different sections over a series of client interactions. Remember that the intent is not to just ask questions, but to use the responses to trigger digital ideation.

For every question, view them through the DAF lens. Evaluate each response against the 11-elements of DAF to see relevance. And for the relevant ones, ask yourself how it will benefit both your client's company and yours.

You can conduct the customer profile mapping exercise on your own, but we have seen it is always better if you do it in a group and often through a workshop after the initial fact finding.

We have divided the customer characterization into 3 parts:
- Customer Demographics
- Customer Empathy
- Sales and Interactions

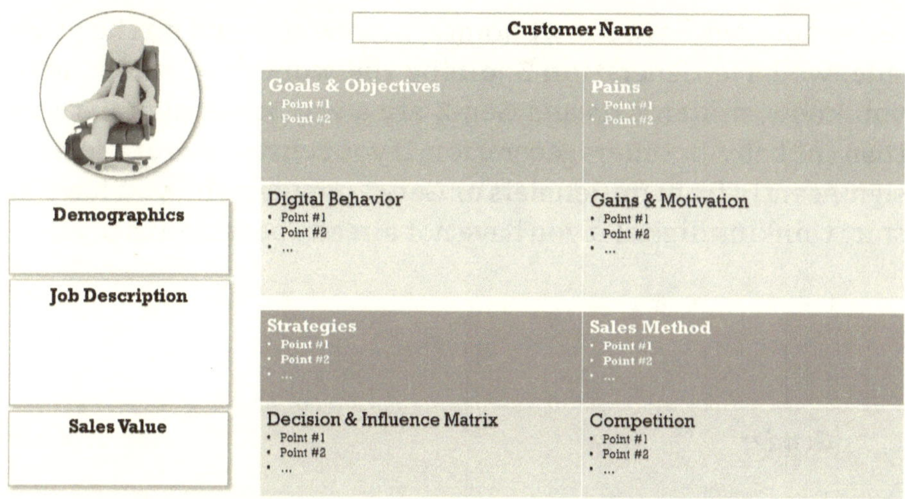

Image: Customer Profile Mapping

Customer Demographics

DEMOGRAPHICS-ROLE IMPACT

Image: Customer Demographics mapping

Age

We are living in remarkably interesting times. Due to delayed retirement, we have baby-boomers on one side and on the other side, we have Generation-Z joining the workforce. As many of you know, millennials and Gen-Z are a way more digital savvy than the baby-boomers generation. If your customers or users are significantly from millennials or Gen-Z populations, you have to start thinking digital if you have not already begun on that path.

Gender

There is a strong equality drive in terms of gender diversity across the globe. Most of these campaigns are driven through digital platforms and they are drawing strong levels of psychological and emotional connections. Therefore, if your company is supporting a gender diversity cause, you should use digital and social media to relay this information to your customers and users.

Marital Status

It may not be officially acknowledged but the perception is that single or divorced people may spend a considerable amount of time on social media, social interaction sites and other online sites. This increased usage also gives them a better understanding about the nuances of the platforms.

Family Details

Parents with teenaged children are more aware of digital apps and platforms. These online platforms — like Khan Academy or Instagram — can be used for teaching mathematics to kids or to capture special moments through photos, respectively. It's not that that other people can not or do not subscribe to these platforms, but individuals with children in teen years are much more likely to be aware of the latest gizmos from the tech world than other groups.

Heritage and Geography background

We live in an increasingly multi-cultural world; you may be born somewhere, your heritage may be from somewhere else and you could be living somewhere else now. People with international connections are much more likely to be on digital and online platforms than the local population. Moreover, these international individuals are also likely to be aware of apps and platforms from their country of heritage as well as from the country where they currently inhabit. People of Chinese heritage who have connections to China, but reside overseas, are likely to be equally adept at WhatsApp as they are on WeChat.

Financial Status

Financial conditions can also drive certain digital behaviors. Apart from indulging an active interest, financial conditions determine if people are able to afford different gadgets for their gaming passions. Given the rapid technological changes, one needs update smartphones every few years, and now with the advent of utility gadgets such as Fitbit, the rate of change is increasingly dramatic.

Longevity with company

How long is your company's tenure with the client? If your client is a long-timer, chances are that they may be set in a certain way of thinking. Most long-timers are adept in their organizational behavior and processes, but struggle with managing transformations. On the other side, they have huge contextual knowledge that can be crucial in developing a digital adoption plan. People who have been with the company for a relatively short period of time are likely to bring in new, fresher ideas from their experience at other companies.

Risk-taker vs Risk-averse

Some people are hardwired to question and challenge everything that comes their way until they are satisfied with the answers before they take any action — especially with new ideas. And then there are others who would jump in as soon as they see the first sign of interest. Organizations need both sets of individuals. Risk-takers are required to initiate transformation, where the risk-averse individuals will be required to ensure completeness of a transformation solution.

Influencer vs Decision Maker

Is your client an influencer or a decision maker? In both cases, they may need a certain level of education and awareness if they want to embark on a digital journey. In fact, many of them may already be exploring online and enhancing their knowledge base. Decision makers of course, would need in-depth but specific information. Market intelligence, digital marketing, business strategy and customer experience can play a key role in their decision making.

Consensus vs Individual Decision Making

Is your client's organization driven by consensus or do some key individuals have the decision making powers? Is there a defined and a transparent process? What are some of the written processes and some of the implicit biases that exist in your client's decision making framework? Is there more importance given to experience and expertise (knowledge marketing) over features and attributes (content marketing)?

Job Description And Nuances

Strategic vs Tactical

Understand your customer's job requirements. How much of their job is strategic and how much of it is tactical? The more strategic their job, the more they will be looking for ideas by which they can grow their company, or make their function more effective with new methods or tools. Those with largely tactical jobs are usually looking for ways to increase their efficiency. In both the cases, there are tons of ways in which you can help them with digital angles. You can talk about digital collaboration tools, you can discuss co-creation and mutual development of products or services and you can ask for their input to enhance their experience.

Collaboration vs Individual

How much of the work of your customer involves collaboration versus being led by individual contribution? There is an acceleration in the surge of collaboration activities over the past 30 years. In the past, collaboration was hindered due to significant usage of paper and drawing boards. With digital collaboration apps such as Trello and Miro, you can foster enterprise-wide collaboration across the globe in real-time. These platforms also can give you the ability to co-create an initiative with your client, such as joint product development. You can also try to participate in one of your customer's programs, which can include creation of consortiums as well as process efficiency programs. The digital world has now opened hundreds of new channels to collaborate.

Leverage external expertise vs in-house

In the past, companies would create a pool of in-house resources to conduct many of their technology programs. With innovations on steroid and displaying huge diversity, it is no longer possible for any organization to maintain all the expertise in-house. Moreover, many requirements tend to be short-term, which removes the need to create a complete in-house team. Instead, your customers need to develop the ability to engage and manage external expertise on their digital journeys. By offering them the solutions to create this expertise, you can be a step ahead of your competition.

Formal authority vs influence

In the past, most companies were structured and functioned in a hierarchical manner. In the digital age, there is a lot more cross-functional team initiatives. While many of your customers would have formal authority, they also need to be adept to use their influence. One of the key requirements of being influential is knowledge. With knowledge marketing and access to key information, you can empower your customers.

Industry leading thinking vs laggard

If your customer belongs to an industry-leading company that has pioneered digital adoption, they provide a rich source of knowledge and experience. By acquiring this, you can help other customers who are behind the curve in terms of adoption. Digital exchange of information, storage and knowledge management are key, especially when you have specific knowledge of certain type of digital adoption. As an example, you can look at usage of digital funnel software or TikTok marketing. If your customers have it, you can learn from them and then share the expertise with other customers.

Market facing vs corporate/HQ centric

Due to the digital adoption, many conventional jobs have also acquired market-facing elements. In the past, only sales, marketing and service delivery people were directly exposed to the clients. Now, with data management, many more people from within your organization are getting exposed to customers either directly or through a digital footprint. How can your company help them to do their jobs better?

Financial & Business case vs innovation & experiments
This is about the depth of digital culture your client's organization has adopted. Are they still planning big, waterfall, business-case centric projects or have they started innovation- and idea-driven experimentation across the organization? By sharing information from your market intelligence and collaborating on ideas, you can help your customers with ideation for their experiments.

Sales Value

Value

While the value of the procurement may not be considered directly relevant to digital ideation, value in relation to other aspects should be considered. Try and understand how your product or service benefits your customer. Understand the context, characterize the benefits and visualize 'What-if' options.

Most people still consider a procurement as a 'transaction'. And this transaction is defined as per 20th century interactions. In the digital age, 'transaction' is being replaced by journey and experience. And this is where you are likely to come across a whole plethora of new digital ideas; user experience through emails, your websites, interaction with your sales, marketing and agents can incubate a rich line-up of ideas.

Value can also be created by extending your product or services through digital appendages. Along with your product, try offering an app, a custom social media community or a software addition; any of these can significantly increase the value of your portfolio.

Number of transactions

Unless you are selling a highly commoditized product through door-to-door sales agents, you are likely to have multiple transactions with your customer. Your regular visits to supermarkets, subscription fees for SaaS, or repeat business with consultants, all give rise to multiple transactions. Each transaction is a potential opportunity for a digital intervention. This can be through data mining that will lead to a better understanding of your customer's buying behavior or it can be in the form of fees related to maintenance.

Decision Process

How is the decision-making process of your client? Is it led by consensus and fact? Do they look for benchmarks? Is there market intelligence to support their decision-making process? Both benchmarks and market intelligence can be handled through digital medium and provides a great opportunity for you to harness. In addition, you can also review the needs and wants of each of the decision maker and accordingly, identify digital components that can appeal to them.

Customer Empathy

CUSTOMER EMPATHY / PSYCHOGRAPHICS

Goals & Objectives
* Cost saving / avoidance
* Growth / new revenue
* Process efficiency
* Cost control
* Digital transformation
* New projects
* New products

Pains
* Costs
* Expertise
* Motivational issues
* Over work
* Unappreciated
* Low salary
* Long hours
* Policies and procedures

Digital Behavior
* Restricted to ERPs
* Internet interaction
* Email interaction and communication
* App usage (personal and professional)
* Collaboration tools usage
* Search usage related to work/projects
* Quest for best practices
* LinkedIn / SM activity

Gains & Motivation
* Recognition and rewards
* Appreciation
* Promotion
* Personal satisfaction
* Inner satisfaction
* Team spirit and inclusion of you
* Company loyalty towards you
* Social impact

Image: Customer Empathy / Psychographics

Goals & Objectives

One of the key components of a job in the modern day is the setting and management of goals and objectives (G&Os) The relative importance of the G&Os for the senior management is much higher than for those at junior levels.

Apart from operational level targets, G&Os may cover a myriad of other targets. For illustration purposes, we have highlighted a few areas that can be trigger digital ideation for you.

Cost saving / avoidance

Every senior manager in companies with cost pressures has cost saving/avoidance targets. This can be an opportunity to introduce RPA (Robotics Process Automation), AI-based services, outsourcing of services, digital marketing, market research and data platform management.

Growth / new revenue

By thinking digital products, services, fulfillment or experience, one can easily provide opportunities for your customers to grow. However, the thinking has to change on your side first; instead of viewing yourself as a pure supplier of products and services, you need to view yourself as a partner in providing services to your customer's customer.

Process efficiency

It is a long foregone conclusion that automation can significantly increase process efficiency. Using modern day tools and technology like artificial intelligence, big-data analytics, and visualization, you can explore a whole range of possibilities with your customer.

Cost control

Business intelligence, market research, UX research, Customer experience, and digital marketing generates huge amounts of data. By mining this data, you create deep insights that can allow you to enhance your cost control measures effectively.

Digital transformation

By understanding your customer's business and behavior, you can pre-empt their needs and recommend ideas that can lead to digital transformation. Remember though that at most times, there is a long lead time before an organization concludes that they need digital transformation. You can play a pivotal role by educating them during the period prior to the conclusion stage and accelerate their journey to reach a conclusion. By being part of their journey, you are likely to develop a level of trust and confidence, which will put you in an excellent position to actually win the digital transformation project.

New projects

Many of the above-mentioned targets will get converted into a structured project, and you can provide digital thinking and resources for these projects. Data analytics, market intelligence and user experience will be a rich source of information for your clients.

New products

These days, almost every product is offered as part of a service instead of being stand-alone. You can play a role to develop certain digital processes to support the new product. The add-ons can be as simple as market research, UX research or digital marketing.

Pains

Apart from understanding the job requirements and goals and objectives of your clients, you must also delve deep into the pain areas of your customers.

Identify and capture areas of pain faced by your customers. Remember first that a large number of pain areas may be implicit in their minds. You may need to ask circumspect questions to get answers to these questions. You may need workshops or interviews or to speak to them informally to extract information on these implicit pain areas. Once identified, use the DAF framework to see if there any relevant elements that can be used to assuage the pains of your customers

Costs

Which costs bother your client the most? Are they not getting the right level of value from their expenditure? Is there a digital way that you can relieve their cost pain areas?

Expertise

There are certain expertise areas where your customers may be weak. This may cause a certain vulnerability for them. If the expertise is linked with digital or online technology, you can think of augmenting their expertise by providing them services or skills.

Motivational issues

Are your customers suffering from motivational issues? Understand what motivates them. What do they feel passionate about?

Overwork

Do you customers appear overworked or even frustrated at times? One of the biggest reasons for somebody to overwork tends to be lack of skills and expertise. By providing them the right tools and skills, you can help to significantly lower the stress.

Unappreciated

Does your customer feel overworked and underpaid? Do they not feel appreciated for their efforts? During many of my sales calls — once I developed a certain level of comfort with my customers — I have seen them open up and discuss their issues. These issues can be a rich source of opportunities that you can play in.

Low salary

When people mention low salary, it is usually a result of other emotional factors. Stress about a rude boss, being under-appreciated or not feeling motivated enough can manifest itself as a complaint on low salaries.

Long hours

Are your clients working long hours? Is there process efficiency that you can help them with to improve time management?

Policies and procedures

Are there policies and procedures in place that frustrate your customers? Of course you may not be able to change the policies of your customer's company, but, if you try to understand the underlying principles on how a certain policy was put in place, it may give you some ideas that can have a digital angle to them.

Digital Behavior

All your customers use certain digital platforms and online applications to help them in their jobs. The tool can be a simple item like a Google search or a complicated AI-powered platform; the range can be vast. It is important for you to create a digital behavior mapping for your customers. This can help you think of digital solutions that you can offer to them.

Restricted to ERPs

Many of your customers may not be very tech-savvy, but since they work in an organization, they would have to use certain technologies such as ERPs, emails, file storage, etc. These are the people who limit their exposure to digital technology to a minimum, need-based level. A certain level of digital education and a bit of hand-holding can take them a long way.

Internet interaction

How much time does your customer spend on the internet — be it purely for entertainment or knowledge upgrade and market intelligence? The more savvy your customers are, the more likely they are to adopt a new technology.

Email interaction and communication

Does your customer use emails as their primary communication or do they use emails to support their physical interactions? One of the services that has seen a tremendous rise in the recent times is the availability of templates and techniques as a service. There are companies that will give you tons of email templates as part of their digital marketing that can be very handy to your customers. In fact, you can create a few templates and share those with them.

App usage (personal and professional)

How savvy are your customers in terms of digital and smartphone apps? People who use apps a lot are also likely to be aware of the underlying principles and business models. This makes them more open to new digital ideas.

Collaboration tools usage

Does your customer use online collaboration tools? Can they work with shared documents that different people work on simultaneously? There are tons of collaboration tools that are available in the market. If you have a collaboration tool, you can definitely share it with your client. If you don't, use a 3rd-party collaboration tool, but do start on some form of collaboration on ideas. Imagine creating a mind-map for a customer pain area and then contributing to it.

Search usage related to work/projects

How much of market research does your customer perform online? Is this an area where you can help?

Quest for best practices

I am sure your customers would have asked you at some point about a best practice that you might have seen. With the amount of information available online, you can easily create a significant market intelligence that you can share with your customers.

LinkedIn / SM activity

Understand the depth and diversity of your customer's social media presence. Are they active? What are their preferred platforms? Depending on their usage, you can start with digital invitations to your online communities, groups and other knowledge centers that your customers can benefit from. Nowadays, companies build communities to create an eco-system with their customers, suppliers, partners and others. This can become a great digital story for you.

Gains & Motivation

Just as job requirements and customer pains can be a rich source of ideas for digital adoption, you must also explore what motivates them, what gains they get from their jobs and what makes them happy.

Recognition and Rewards

There is no better motivation that recognition and rewards. In fact, studies suggest that recognition has a bigger impact on motivation than financial gains. Recognition is seen as a validation of the efforts of an employee. And it also creates a certain credibility within the organization. By conferring recognition, a company also asserts its faith and displays confidence in the capability of an individual.

Every organization has their own methods to recognize and reward their employees, but there is one common trend. Individuals who put in a lot of effort in their roles, who go and up and beyond their job requirements, and who find innovative ways to get things done are usually the ones who get recognized. Getting work done more efficiently, saving costs and increasing productivity are a few examples. Digital innovation can play significant role in any of these efforts.

Appreciation

Usually organization follow a process for rewards and recognition. There is only a limited number of people who are selected for this process. Rewards and recognition are also conferred for consistent effort rather than for a single achievement. On the other side, individual efforts can be appreciated for each activity. This appreciation can be from your boss, your peers or from your subordinates. Thinking outside the box or coming up with suggestions by which daily operations can be improved are a few ways in which people can get appreciation.

Promotion

What is the criteria followed by organizations to promote staff? What is the criteria for senior positions? When you look deeply into these measures, you will find that a large number of people are promoted on the basis of their efforts to bring in new growth, cost efficiencies, team motivation and getting work done. By analyzing the conditions, you can make several digital adoption suggestions to your client.

Personal satisfaction

What makes your customers satisfied in their jobs? Is it jobs done on-time, within budget, employee satisfaction, or other conditions that drive satisfaction? There are multiple ways by which satisfaction can be driven. Every manager derives a certain level of satisfaction when they can do their jobs better, faster and more efficient.

Inner satisfaction

There is subtle difference between personal satisfaction and inner satisfaction. Personal satisfaction can be transactional and may involve an activity from your clients' daily operations. Inner satisfaction on the other hand is about delivering what your client feels passionately about. This can in terms of social impact, a certain philosophy or a belief, religion in some cases or it could be a sport. Whatever the item is, it has a strong appeal to this person. By exploring what your clients feel passionate about, you can think of ideas that can drive digital adoption. Social media expression, story-telling for content generation, and improved user experience are just a few examples.

Team spirit and inclusion of you

Collaboration, team spirit and definitive inclusion of 'you' in an initiative or a program can be a huge motivation for an individual. Most of you would remember times when you felt that you were left out of a certain program, and how discouraged you felt at that time. The power of inclusion is a huge gain driver. Now, let us be honest, you can not be included in everything. Nor would you be included if you did not do or think anything differently. One of the ways to increase your chance of getting included in teams, boards and focus groups, can be driven by ideation. You can regularly equip your customers with ideas, market intelligence and content.

Company loyalty towards you

Employees can experiment and take risks when they can think freely and are assured of their company's faith in them. In order to encourage innovation and new ideation, companies must show a certain level of loyalty towards you. Only then will you feel safe to voice your opinion and start experimenting. One must remember that most experiments are going to fail. This is important fact to realise. Unfortunately, many companies forget that the reason why most experiments fail is to do with uncertainties rather than people making mistakes. People regularly get reprimanded in many organizations when experiments fail. As your client is likely to be in a position of influence, you have a wonderful chance to educate them and potentially prepare them for a digital culture.

Social impact

Given the higher awareness of social evils and prevailing bigoted practices, more people are getting involved with social impact initiatives. These can be as simple as donating regularly to charity organizations for preventing animal cruelty or can be actively supporting a certain cause. There is a high probability that most of your clients also have a social impact cause that you may not be aware of. Try and discover more on this aspect. Like other gain and motivational items, social impact support may play a significant role in the lives of your client. And with your market intelligence, digital culture and user experience, you can indeed create additional loyalty from your clients. That is why many services'/ products' companies have started including social causes as part of their activities, including allocating a certain portion of their revenue to the cause.

Sales And Interactions

INTERACTION & SALES IDEATION TRIGGERS

Strategies	Sales Method
• Sales strategy / method • Marketing efforts • Freebies • Knowledge sharing	• Direct interaction • Email • Social call • Event invitation • Information and blogs sharing • White paper sharing
Decision & Influence Matrix	**Competition**
• How are you influencing decisions • Do you know all the parties at your clients organization • Is decision making criteria transparent • Do all the decision makers and influencers have the right awareness • Do all the decision makers and influencers have the right expertise • How are they educated and trained • How do they get knowledge	• Competition strategy • How is your competition influencing your client • How are they sharing knowledge and best practices • How are their digital interactions with your client • How is your competition's digital presence • Include strategic elements from your customers, suppliers and other partners

Image: Customer Sales Interaction

Strategies

Companies deploy different strategies for interaction with existing and potential customers. Earlier, it was primarily the sales guys who would interact with the customers and sometimes, people in the marketing or product teams. With digital marketing and digital customer experience, the number of interactions between customers and your online-present assets have grown exponentially.

Sales strategy / method

Before the digital proliferation, most of the interactions with customers and prospects were based on features and characteristics of your products and services. Now, with so many digital players and unbelievable product offerings, it is no longer enough to sell by just sharing features and characteristics. Present day prospects do not want just your product; they want you to solve their problems with your products and services. There is a tectonic shift in the way sales must be conducted now.

Marketing efforts

As you know, only a small number of leads eventually convert to sales. So, bigger the leads base is, the more sales you will generate. With digital and online marketing, you can now reach out to thousands of more prospects, which can lead to a significantly larger number of leads.

Freebies

Until the 90s, information was considered a premium asset. Now, with so much of information available online, the new differentiator is experience. And the only way in which people buy a new product or a service is by actually experiencing it. With cloud computing, secured online payments and digital marketing, companies regularly offer free trials, scaled-down products for free or massively discounted, bundled products to give potential customers an experience with their products. There are also companies who continue to offer their main product for free and only charge for any up-sell items.

Knowledge sharing

Along with experience, the other crucial change in customer behavior is the use of own experience and insights to generate high quality content. One massive advantage with knowledge sharing is that it creates instant credibility and the knowledge asset often becomes a magnet for lead generation. A case in point being templates and ebooks for download are being regularly used for knowledge marketing. One of the best examples is an actual published book. With the new self-publishing solutions now available, this highly effective tool is now being used for knowledge marketing.

Sales Method

In the previous section, we talked about various sales strategies, in this section, we will talk about the actual tactics deployed during interactions with your customer and prospects.

Direct interaction

Until a few years ago, most sales calls were primarily social in nature. With the explosion in digital interactions, the number of direct interactions has lowered quite significantly. Moreover, customers have started demanding more concrete discussions during their interactions vis-à-vis a social call. Many of my sales colleagues use a phone call or a WhatsApp chat for social engagement and actual physical meetings for concrete discussions. A new art form is developing now, on how to manage customer 'relationships' through a digital medium.

Email

Apart from on transactions, many sales and marketing teams are using emails to share information and create awareness about new products and services. An email can be quite effective in terms of sharing insights and educating your customers. Caution needs to be exercised regarding the email interactions in terms of frequency and content. In their eagerness to share a lot of information and product features, inadvertently many people crossover to the spamming side.

Social call

While social calls are still widely used for interaction with potential and existing customers, some of the activities prior to a meeting can be conducted through a digital medium. This can be in terms of sending your customers a link to your PDF download or sharing a trial version prior to your social call.

Event invitation

Most event invitations these days go through a digital medium. Whether you use Mailerlite, Mailchimp or other email applications, you now get access to tons of data. With professional event management softwares and email applications, you can now easily figure out details like who opened your email, who clicked on the links that you shared, people who registered and so forth, Based on the data analysis, you can tweak your campaign, and in some cases, even your event.

Information and blog sharing

Content marketing is a big part of any company's marketing effort. By including information about tools and applications, usage, case studies and blogs, you can increase the readability of your content. Since most of the content is online, you can also understand your customer's behavior and affinity towards your product. Analyzing your customer's digital interactions can prepare you to have more informed and targeted conversations.

White paper sharing

I have called out this element separately from the above on account of the fact that white papers tend to be much more elaborate and comprehensive than blogs in dealing with a topic. While a blog may span a couple of pages at most, most of the good white papers run into several pages with rich content. White papers are a great way to showcase your credibility and experience, in addition to being a tool for educating your customers.

Decision & Influence Matrix

Decision making in most organizations is no longer a single event; it is a process. This process follows a sequence of starting out with recognition of a problem and ends with a purchase order for a product or service. During this journey, the process touches multiple parties, it imparts some level of education and it includes influencing others to drive consent before arriving at a decision. During the process, a certain level of background and market intelligence may be carried out to substantiate the arguments.

How are you influencing decisions?

Try and get an understanding about the factors that your client may consider for decision making. Extend this thought process by delving deeper on the factors, which may not be explicitly spelt out but may be used to drive — and sometimes bias — decision-making through influence. Market intelligence, user experience, organization capabilities, knowledge marketing and digital culture may play a differentiating role in influencing the decision.

Do you know all the parties at your client's organization?

In consensus buying, many sales teams get lulled by the satisfied interaction with their liaison in an organization and miss out on critical input from other parties. While mapping your client's decision making matrix is important, it is more important to understand how they are getting their knowledge and education to help them drive their decision making.

Are the decision making criteria transparent?

These days, many organizations claim to have a transparent process. In reality, much of the mechanics is actually made transparent to support the claim. When it comes to setting context and education of key decision makers, the softer aspects are not necessarily transparently covered. These unwritten rules and softer guidelines provide a significant opportunity for organizations to use their knowledge marketing and digital marketing to influence the decision making process.

Do all decision makers and influencers have the right awareness?

The pace of changes in technology and business processes in the past used to be more gradual than the changes we see in the digital age. In the past, you would have a significant amount of learning on-the-job. Today's tech changes do not allow that luxury; you will need to make additional efforts to get yourself educated and be made aware of these tech changes.

Do all decision makers and influencers have the right expertise?

Expertise takes the earlier point of awareness a notch up. Just knowing how artificial intelligence works does not make you an expert. You must have a depth of understanding by which you can draw a relevance or fit-for-purpose conclusion and utilize critical thinking to draw up potential solutions, and ability to make prudent decisions. Market intelligence and digital management can be great sources to develop expertise.

How are they educated and trained?

It is one thing to get on-the-job training and awareness, and quite another to acquire specialised skills through focused training and education. As a service provider, this gives you a massive opportunity to bridge the gap and create customized training for your customers.

How do they acquire knowledge?

Newsletters, blogs, videos, webinars, online training, seminars, magazines, books and online reference websites are just a few examples by which your client can upgrade their knowledge. Quite often, many of your clients may not be mentally oriented on how to extract information in a manageable way. By giving them byte-sized information nuggets, you can share your knowledge and enhance their understanding of the subject.

Competition

Understanding and preparing for competition is an essential element of existence of any business. Just as you are constantly focusing on your competition, your customers are also focusing on their rivals all the time. Many companies fail to notice the importance of your client's competition and only try to focus on the functional requirements of your customers and your own operations. Understanding and advising your customer on their competition can certainly bring a level of trust and with add an edge to your business.

Competition strategy

It may not be easy to get access to your client's strategic play-book. However, if you create a list of specific questions about their strategy, it may be easier to get answers directly. How will your clients address their competition? How are they planning to gain market share? Are they exploring any potential collaborations? Most importantly, are they planning to develop a new product or service? And is there a way that you can play a role in the development of their new product or services, and is there a digital play?

How is your competition influencing your client?

In hyper-competitive markets, competition pushes companies to either play a price game or send them towards innovation. How is your competition influencing your client's tactics and operations? Your client may be looking for new business strategies or operational efficiencies. Have your competitors already made inroads into those initiatives? In a majority of these cases, you should be able to contribute to those discussions.

How is your competition sharing knowledge and best practices?

What is the mechanism by which your competition is providing information and best practices to your client? How are they sharing their knowledge — via training, videos, blogs, whitepapers, consultants, etc.? How does your client verify those information nuggets? And is there an active validation initiative that your client has embarked on with your competitor?

How are their digital interactions with your client?

How are your competitors interacting with your client? Is it primarily through physical world interactions? What sort of digital mediums are they using to interact with your customers? What kind of information are they sharing through these channels? What measures are they taking to improve their customer online experience?

How is your competition's digital presence?

Do your competitors have digital components of their products and services? How active are these components? Are these a full product or a service, or are they part of order fulfilment? What is your competitors' intensity of the focus on online presence? By analyzing your competition's online environments, you can conjure a large number of ideas on how your company can boost its online effectiveness.

Include strategic elements from your customers, suppliers, other partners
All the elements that I covered under the competition subsection can also be extended to other parties, including suppliers, partners, distributors, affiliates and others. Ask similar questions like the ones above: What is their digital strategy? How are they faring against their own competition? Are they focusing on digital marketing? Is user experience high on their agenda? Try and observe what they are doing, analyze and learn from those examples. And if they are relevant, adopt them.

Wrapping Up

As mentioned at the opening of this chapter, most sound strategies start with customers. I have extended the same thinking to digital ideation. By observing and studying your customer's empathy, you will get a deep understanding of their characteristics and behavior. Once you reach that stage of comprehension, you will also realize that many of your customer's needs could well have digital solutions. That is where the power of this exercise lies. The truth is I have shared a secret technic here with you. But you have to act upon it quickly. Remember, there will always be somebody else out there who is already acting it!

100+ DAF IDEAS BASED ON 6M+

The 6M (Man, Machine, Mother Nature, Measurement, Method, Material) method is widely used as a cause-and-effect analysis tool. And it is easy to see why. It provides a comprehensive thinking approach to find causes that create a certain effect. In this method, for a given 'effect', the team is asked to identify causes under each of the 'M' categories. By proving different 'M's, teams get hooks based on which they can broaden their thinking.

Practitioners across the globe use the 6M method consistently in projects including LEAN six-sigma. Be it a process improvement project or a new product introduction, the 6M tool provides a strong base for analysis.

I had my first exposure to this method during my LEAN six-sigma days in General Electric. I found it highly effective and it became one of the favorite tools of my professional toolkit. Being a cross-pollinator myself, I experimented this framework in other disciplines, including Ideation, as it uses lateral thinking faculties.

Over the years, I have added a few more elements to the frame-

work for the purposes of ideation to create an 11-element idea-tion tool:
- Person (Man)
- Machine
- Environment (Mother Nature)
- Measurement
- Method
- Material
- Organization & Culture
- Leadership
- Governance & Management
- Communication
- Strategy

Person (Man)

This refers to all individuals that are part of the ecosystem and who have definite roles to play. These could be individual contributors, front-line workers, line managers or they could be suppli-ers, customers, partners, contractors. We distinguish them from leadership as the 'person' group work in the business whereas the leadership — in this case, executive leadership or the CXO team — work on the business.

In terms of digital thinking, you must think of the following elements:
- Customer experience
- Supplier experience
- Partner experience
- Digital marketing for customers and prospects
- Who from your organization should participate for inter-actions on the digital medium
- Operations
- Experience

- Matrix and KPIs on interactions
- Technical support
- Multi-channel presence management
- Channel interaction
- Knowledge marketing

These are just few ideas to get your creative thinking going.

Machine

We will refer to any kind of technology in this category. This can be items such as laptops, smartphones, scanners or storage devices. They could also include digital concepts like cloud-computing as well as software. And not forget chatbots, robots and other enabling technologies — also part of this group.

From an ideation perspective, you should ideate on:
- Collaboration software
- Chatbots
- Intelligent and Enterprise AI based solutions
- Big data analytics
- IoT (Internet of Things)
- Blockchain as multi-party system
- Cloud-computing for scale-up and flexibility

In addition, you should dive further into:
- Smartphone apps
- Software-as-a-service
- Subscriptions

Environment (Mother Nature)

This is a broad category that includes your workplace, your marketplace, your industry as well as your home. In today's world, digital presence is everywhere and can influence various aspects of the world around you.

Here are a few ideas under this category to think about:
- Collaboration amongst teams
- Ecommerce
- E-sourcing
- Industry webinars
- Digital events

You can also include enabling technologies that help:
- Workplace
- Home offices
- Communication

Measurement

With so much of digital footprint across devices and physical spaces, data is the new gold. But there is so much of it in hidden form that it can become overwhelming very quickly. Remember that the final objective is not just about generating data, it is also about effectively collecting it, mining it and creating meaningful insights out of it.

If you do digital marketing, you would be generating humongous amounts of data. On the face of it, the sheer volume and kinds of the data can look very attractive. But once you start measuring them is when you realize its actual effectiveness. As an example, many companies measure the number of clicks on their newsletters. Now, imagine that your newsletter has multiple buttons as well as multiple social media icon shares. You will soon have to think which clicks must you meas-ure and which ones can be set on a lower priority.

As some examples, here are some of various items that you can measure:
- Number of clicks
- Number of email opens
- Amount of time spent
- Buyer conversion
- Number of downloads
- Number of attendees in a digital event
- Number of leads generated through lead magnet

The trick is narrowing down what it is in the digital environment that you want to measure and why. Once you have ascertained that, you should then think of how to manage it effectively.

Method

Method can be described either as an approach or a process. For sporadic usage or for project management, you can refer to it as an approach. LEAN management is an approach, for instance. DMAIC is a six-sigma project approach. Agile and Scrum are actively used as approaches in digital companies.

Process will be described as a series of repeatable steps that have been codified. They can be order fulfilment, customer acquisition, lead generation or it could be user interactions, prospect educa-tion and many others.

Digital technology can be used as your product or in your products. It can also be an integral part of your service. But more importantly, now, all your user interactions can be converted into digital processes. They would include user experience (UX), social media interactions or knowledge mar-keting processes.

This category should be able to generate more ideas compared to the others for digital adoption:
- Order fulfilment journey
- Customer acquisition journey
- Market awareness and education
- Digital channel interactions
- Digital marketing (AIDA)
- Lead magnet management and lead generation
- Customer engagement
- User experience enhancement
- Subscriber management
- Knowledge marketing approaches

Material

In the old-economy businesses, material was referred to physical material that was used for construction, manufacturing and production. These could be items such as chemicals, products or raw material such as petroleum, plant resins, among others.

In the digital age, this category can be extended to cover software, digital codes as well as doc-uments, digital files and other online material.

Digital companies should focus on online material, including eBooks, trial software, tools and templates under the category:
- Form of software distribution
- User manuals
- System documentation
- Pdf downloads
- eBooks
- Digital reports
- Online magazine
- Bundled tools and templates

Organization & Culture

Organizational management for a digital company needs entirely different methods and cul-ture, and many companies around the globe have struggled — and some are still wrestling — to bridge the gap. They want to use technology of the digital age but their management teams are still immovably entrenched in the 20th century mindset.

Digital enterprises must be conceptualized as either digital assembly lines or should be viewed as data production organizations. And getting to this new visualization warrants a fundamental change in management thinking. Digital organizations must have a culture is all about continuous innovation and experimentation. These requirements need specialized skills — not just in technology but also in people with strong lateral thinking. This culture also needs openness, transparency and empowerment across all levels of organization.

Under organization, the following elements must be considered:
- Leadership team skills and education
- Digital catalyst leaders
- Change management
- Culture of experiments
- Experiment coordination function
- Center of Expertise management
- Enterprise-wide mass Training and education
- Agile and scrum approach

Leadership

New-age organizations must be led from the front by digital-savvy leaders who have a good understanding of the different digital technology and are well aware of the techniques by which the digital power can be unlocked. As it is humanly impossible to be a master of all these new technologies, the new-age digital leader must be capable of engaging and collaborating with internal and external parties to adopt new technology solutions.

Executive leadership as well as mid-level management must place special emphasis on digital adoption, including developing:
- Leadership team skills and education
- Digital catalyst leaders
- Tools and templates
- Career progression
- New digital and data departments

Governance & Management

As is the case with any transformation project, the entire journey of capability may take 12-18 months. During the transition, and in the steady-state, organizations must review the follow-ing aspects:
- Operational management framework
- Performance indicators and metrics
- Operational rigor
- Steering committee and management overview
- Management reporting
- Operational calendar
- Resource management

Communication

Communication is one aspect that gets covered in all other areas and yet, in any digital adop-tion program, it forms a key component of the transformation journey. Starting from initiation, ideation all the way to implementation and steady-state, clear and consistent communication is required at all times.

In digital projects, the following must be considered:
- Collaboration tools
- Employee communication
- External party communication
- Medium of communication
- Social media management
- Digital marketing management
- Knowledge management
- User and Customer experience management

Strategy

Many companies bring about changes and structures based merely on current organization, whereas for a truly effective transformation journey, current state, transition state and future state must all be considered. In case of digital adoption, due to high levels of uncertainty, ex-perimentation and hypothesis-usage, organizations must embrace certain specific strategic elements in their thinking.

Organizations must consider the following:
- Structure to manage "pivot-or-persevere"
- LEAN startup
- Continuous usage of minimum viable product (MVP principles)
- Scale-up
- Agile thinking including user stories, product management and sprints
- Agile based rolling wave capability building.

Wrapping-Up

So, this was the 11-element ideation engine. I have shared multiple angles for each element. You should read and identify the relevant items that can be used for your organization. By conducting the 100-idea session across various teams and departments, you could easily create a rich reposi-tory of ideas. Remember, most organizations do not have enough ideas to work with, and with the 100-idea repository, you will be spoilt for choice.

CLOSING REMARKS

In this book, we have covered a lot of ground on ideation from digital adoption. First, we started with understanding the pre-condition that can create fertile grounds for ideation. Stagnant growth is a good starting point. Secondly, we discussed the digital trends that will define the way we conduct business in the 2020s. These trends are amplifying the need to go digital immensely. Thirdly, we spoke about the need to actually acknowledge and align the organization on acceptance of the problem and potential solution directions.

We then introduced the 11-element digital adoption framework (DAF). DAF is used to dissect the digital requirements into functional and operational parts. This dissection helps organizations to think and ideate comprehensively on digital adoption.

Customer understanding is one of the pillars of any good digital ideation. We first spoke about various customers, prospects and users that are part of your business universe. And then delved deep into your customer's empathy and psychographics mapping.

With DAF and good understanding of your customer requirements, we then embarked on deep ideation through 6M+ model. This 100+ ideation approach is to ensure that you can create a massive repository of ideas on one side, and approach customer and operational requirements from various angles to look for potential digital solutions.

But I must say here that having a good ideation framework is not enough. Here are a few points that I would like you to remember when you embark on your ideation process.

Digital Savvy Leadership

Digital adoption is not for the fainthearted. While it starts with technology, the real benefit is extracted when you unleash functional power of digital technologies to resolve most painful business problems. Not only would your teams need good understanding about the involved technologies, there is a significant amount of change management and leadership drive that is a prerequisite for successful digital adoption. Your digitally savvy leadership should both understand the power of technology and acutely understand the problem areas of your business where these technologies can be used. They should also, understand a need to bring cultural change in your organization. They must lead the initiative from the front.

Culture Of Experiment

For any successful digital adoption, a company must have a strong culture of experimentation. If you have been in a risk-averse business, then you have to start taking risks and become an innovative company. Instead of focusing on desktop business cases, and death by PowerPoint presentations, you need to cultivate a culture where everybody is free to share ideas and participate in experiments. The culture needs to permeate across different layers of your company. Individuals must be able to generate hundreds of ideas and conduct experiments in an open and encouraging environment.

Agile

When you embark on a digital adoption journey, there are a lot of uncertainties that exist. During your journey you will discover new things that will require you to modify and course correct your direction. All of this cannot be predicted or estimated up-front. To have lengthy preparations for creating project plans or business cases, is not practical. Rapid innovation and large-scale experimentation would need a certain degree of agility in the organization. Given the usual circumstances, we strongly recommend agile and lean startup methods to be deployed during digital adoption journeys. Managing through user stories and sprints will significantly improve your chances of a successful adoption.

Engage Experts

There are several components of digital technology where you will need specific expertise to implement. In the past, companies would invest heavily in creating this expertise in-house. With rapid technology changes, it has now become virtually impossible to maintain high-caliber individuals on your payroll. Most digital companies have now created an eco-system of internal resources alongside a pool of external experts who collaborate on a regular basis. It is no longer a stigma to engage external experts. In fact, it is prudent, it costs less and provides tremendous flexibility to create your own eco-system of experts. That is why, it is important that your company starts thinking along those lines as well.

Process Of Ideation

Every business has their own unique requirements. This ideation book is to provide you with a structured thinking approach on how to generate huge number of ideas in a short period of time. For the first time in our living history, we are faced with a situation where the future of businesses have become highly uncertain. Under these circumstances, every business has to generate ideas constantly and in large numbers all the time, in order to create and maintain a competitive advantage. Thus, every organization must institutionalize the process of digital ideation and innovation in their operations.

Finally, every new business concept and framework only gets better with usage and application. I will be keen to hear from you about your experiences and learn from you on how you have gone about implementing the ideas from this book. So, do drop me a line and tell me about them.

Wishing you a great Digital Adoption journey!

ACKNOWLEDGEMENT

I would like to thank my wife, Devyani Sen who stood by me during this crazy phase of writing this book as well as her help in the initial editing of the book. She helped me distill thousands of ideas before I could write the book.

I would like to thank my editor Nupur Chakraborty without whom the book would be incomplete and incongruent. Your persistant support and advice on how to put down my experiences in words has been a great support throughout the process of writing this book.

And finally, I would like to thank my family who have stood by me through this process.

BOOKS BY THIS AUTHOR

Right-Fit Digital Strategy To Accelerate Growth

This is the decade when most businesses will become digital. It does not matter whether you are a logistics business, a training company, a retail business or a consulting business, most of the activities of your company are going to be conducted on a digital medium.

With so many people being online and companies adopting novel ways to connect with customers and even prospective buyers using enabling technologies, it has become imperative that all businesses must have a digital strategy.

Even with a good understanding of enabling technologies, businesses fight with finding the right applications within their organization. The bridge between theory and relevance is often a bridge too far. But innovation always finds its way through.

What is your digital strategy? What is your competitive advantage story? How are you going to service and support your customers as well as prospects?

Digital adoption is not a binary change. In this book, we have introduced an 11-elements Digital Adoption Framework on various digital innovations usage focused on business growth ranging from user experience, digital marketing, knowledge marketing to being a complete digital and data organization. This framework will allow you to convert your digital aspirations into manageable chunks of tactical approaches.

This book will provide you a structured approach on how to adopt digital technology seamlessly and unlock opportunities that will put your business on a high growth trajectory.